For Jennene Stanley, my creative friend who eats "can't" for breakfast. You inspire me every day!

and

For Gwynne Beneke, UCO's faculty advisor and founder of New Plains Review. Your invitation to participate in the brand-new Liberal Arts magazine started my path!

PRAISE FOR PEGGY DOVIAK

"As practical as it is inspirational, (Doviak) has drawn on her many years of working closely with financial planning clients to make personal finance lively and compelling. . . . Peggy puts the consumer first, knowing that the best financial advice is never absolute, one-size-fits-all."

— ELEANOR BLAYNEY, CFP® RETIRED
CONSUMER ADVOCATE FOR CFP BOARD

"Cheers to Peggy for a tutorial about finance that didn't put me to sleep!"

— AMAZON REVIEWER

"Peggy makes it so simple to read, follow and take simple steps to financial freedom, NO MATTER where you are in the journey. . . . I have never found a financial book that was simple to digest until now."

— AMAZON REVIEWER

52 WEEKS TO FEARLESS

WHAT CREATIVES NEED TO KNOW ABOUT MONEY

PEGGY DOVIAK

CENTERBOARD PRESS

Centerboard Press
Norman, Oklahoma

Paperback edition printed in the United States | First Edition March 2025

ISBN: 979-8-218-59432-9

Library of Congress Control Number: 2025901595

For information on paperback orders:
peggy@peggydoviak.com

DISCLAIMER

The information in this book is educational in nature and not investment advice. Consult any strategy with your own financial team before you implement it. Investing is risky, and you can lose money.

Additionally, any time the terms "financial planner" or "planner" are used, the assumption is the author is referring to a CERTIFIED FINANCIAL PLANNER™ practitioner.

TABLE OF CONTENTS

Investment Chapters

Retirement

Taxes

Estate

Other

Part II

1
WELCOME!

*M*oney can be overwhelming, scary, and confusing. People in financial services can also be intimidating and, sometimes, condescending. Worse than that, sometimes worrying about money can seem at odds with being a creative. You want to focus on your art, and spending time exploring your finances can almost feel like you are selling out.

If any of these sentences resonate with you, I have good news. I understand. I've written this book for you. Together, we will look at money in organic and empowering ways.

Before I go further, I want to talk about my background. In high school, I wanted to be a concert pianist; however, I majored in English in college rather than music. I also earned a master's in creative studies, focusing on creative writing. Music has remained an important part of my life through church and community events. Additionally, I have edited fiction and nonfiction and have published several books. I am a creative who owns a financial planning firm.

I became so angry with a stockbroker who took advantage of my mother that I entered the field of finance. It was a stunning career shift, but I'm glad I did it. I enjoy helping people understand their money. I particularly resonate with folks who don't like numbers and finance.

Although some of you may enjoy following the stock market or balancing your bank statements, I suspect many do not. I wrote this book for you. Everyone needs to understand their money.

I am beginning this book with an important assumption: You aren't abandoning your creative side if you worry about having enough money. The "starving artist" may be a common stereotype, but it's unhealthy and unfair to you. Understanding money doesn't mean you are ruled by it. Paying off your bills and saving for retirement are noble goals, no matter what you do for a living.

This book is written for people in different artistic genres. I try to use examples that relate to all kinds of creatives. I will also give you an activity at the end of each chapter, so you can apply the information I've discussed.

First, a few words on how I organized the material. Roughly, the first half of the book covers topics that all creatives need to know about money. I categorized them the same way the CFP® Board of Standards divides the topics: Cash flow, Insurance, Investments, Retirement, Taxes, and Estate. I also added an "Other" section to include issues I thought you might find interesting.

The second half of the book is specifically written for creatives who want to treat their endeavors like a business. These topics include information on business structures, marketing, taxes, and other issues. Choosing where to put some of the topics was challenging, and I would encourage you to skim the second half of the book even if you don't want to open a business. You will still find useful information.

Because all the topics are complex, I want you to think of

this book as an introduction to the information. You will probably need to read more details about the individual topics, but this book gives you a place to start. Note: I can't give investment advice in a book, because I don't know your circumstances. All the information is educational only. Talk to your own financial team—your planner or adviser, your CPA, and your attorney—for more information that will apply to you.

Finally, people sometimes ask me why I write financial books with fifty-two chapters. With fifty-two weeks in a year, you only need to read one chapter a week to finish. Don't worry. The chapters aren't long. After a year, you will have many strategies you can use to lower your stress and gain control of your money. Let's get started!

Activity

Think about your financial life. What would make it easier? On the following lines, write down two or three specific financial goals you have. As you learn solutions, return to these pages and write down the chapter numbers and actions you can take to improve things.

_____

_____

_____

_____

PART I

MONEY AND YOUR LIFE

52

CASH FLOW CHAPTERS

2

TRACK YOUR SPENDING

*B*y the end of the month, the money was gone. Bonnie tried to save some of what she earned as a studio musician, but she wasn't very successful. One month, she'd put a little back, but the next month, she would need it. She didn't know how to break the cycle.

If you want to spend your energy on creative pursuits, you may not have as much time to work in a traditional career, in a job that pays you every two weeks with regularity. The transition from employee to entrepreneur can be scary. Before you make the leap, look at your cash flow, your money in and money out. I like the term "cash flow" more than "budget," because budgets make people break out in hives. Instead, I'm just concerned that you have enough income every month to pay your bills.

Many people believe that their net worth, or the value of all their possessions minus their debt, determines their financial success. On one level, it's true. As your net worth increases, your debt is decreasing, your assets are increasing, or you are saving more. Net worth is a valuable measurement, but I believe that people live and die by their cash flow.

Your monthly financial situation should ensure you can meet your obligations and goals.

If you regularly spend more than you earn, you are either eating away at your savings or accruing debt. Either occurrence is dangerous.

Your savings forms the backbone of your emergency fund, an important topic we will discuss in a later chapter. Additionally, consumer debt, or credit card debt, can become financially crippling, especially in today's higher interest rate environment. When interest creates an additional twenty to thirty percent liability, the balance becomes almost impossible to eliminate.

Many people tell me they don't know how their credit card balances climb. I suspect that statement isn't entirely true. I think they know why the balances increase; they just don't know what to do about it.

At a basic level, debt increases when we spend more than we earn. The best first step to get control of this situation is to know your monthly expenses. By tracking every dime you spend during the month, you can see where your money is going,

I think tracking your spending is a valuable exercise. I've done it myself during times of financial change. I wanted to transition from a job that paid me a salary every two weeks to working full-time in my new financial firm whose bills exceeded its income. To avoid disaster, I tracked my husband's and my spending. I needed to be sure we could live on his salary and pay for the additional bills I had added to our household.

When you track your spending for a month, you may come to the same conclusion I did. I was certain we didn't spend that much. To prove myself correct, I tracked our spending for a second month. Surprisingly, we spent that much again.

I faced the horrifying realization that my husband and I spent a lot of money. Our basic bills were fine, but we liked to eat out. A lot. I discovered that if we cut our food bill, we could live on his salary. Then, I could work full-time in my financial firm. My solution was learning to cook. Although I wasn't initially thrilled, cooking has proven to be highly rewarding as I've learned about the spices and flavors of different cultures.

If you want to spend more time in your creative venture, you should begin by knowing what you spend every month. If you dedicate more of your time to your craft, which leads to your initially earning less money, can you pay your bills? Could you spend less and still live a fulfilling life? You have many questions to answer and should look for ingenious solutions. But begin by knowing what you spend.

Activity

For one month, write down everything you spend. Don't skip inexpensive purchases like fast food or coffee. For this month, label the spending as necessary costs or things you could skip. If you are like most people, at the end of thirty days, you will think that your monthly expenses were abnormally high. If so, track your costs for a second thirty days or even a third. You need to know where your money is going before you can decide how to manage it. Jot your notes on the following lines.

_____

_____

3
GOALS TO DREAMS

*J*amie had danced since she was three years old. Now, just out of college, she was getting paid roles in musical theater. She wondered if dance could be her full-time career. It was her dream, but she didn't want to make a mistake. What steps should she take to see if it was financially possible?

Most people who create are dreamers. They see and hear things others cannot. They believe in possibilities and are often not afraid to take risks. I believe in dreams. I think you cannot achieve anything higher than your aim. However, sometimes, having a dream isn't enough. You need to know how to accomplish it. To achieve a dream, you need to have a goal.

Where dreams are abstract and vague, goals are measurable. Maybe you want to be a visual artist with a permanent display in a gallery. Perhaps you're a musician who wants to be part of an orchestra. Maybe you want to quit your day job and become a full-time creative. None of these dreams can occur unless you are more specific.

Let's take a closer look at the goal of quitting your job to pursue your creative endeavor full time. That's the dream. To turn it into a goal, you need to break it into measurable pieces and use some information we already gathered.

Remember when we measured everything you spent? Before quitting your job, you should track your spending for an extended period to ensure your analysis is correct. You don't want to assume you only spend $4,000 a month because you did it once. Down the road, you might discover you usually spend $5,000. That error often leads to credit card debt. If your financial instability gets too extreme, you might even need to declare bankruptcy. If you are considering quitting your job, be sure you know how much you spend.

If you're in a relationship and your partner pays most of the bills, you still need to complete this exercise. Can you survive on only that income? Are they on board with the change in the finances? You shouldn't assume your partner's opinion. Money arguments are the leading cause of divorce, and you should be sure you are both on the same page before you take any major action with your finances.

The second step in turning this dream into a goal is to calculate how much money you can expect to earn each month. When I help people with this, I often see wishcasting.

They say something like, "I'm just about to get a contract/commission/part-time gig that will bring in enough." When I try to help them get specific about the anticipated income, they provide a number that is a large portion of the shortfall.

Here's the problem with that scenario. The amount of money they need isn't income already being earned. Instead, it's a deal that's just about to happen. If you build your finances on expected income, you're in danger if you don't earn it. You might not get the gig, or it may not pay as much as you anticipated. If you want to quit your job, you need to be as certain as possible that you have enough money coming in.

Maybe, after these calculations, you aren't ready to quit your other job yet. That's okay. It brings you to the third part of turning a dream into a goal. How long should you wait to change from a daily job to a creative pursuit? The answer is however long it takes you to be financially secure. By knowing how much money you need, how much money you currently have, and how long it will take you to increase your earnings, your dream has become a goal. Now, you can take the steps to accomplish it.

Activity

Do you have big dreams? That's awesome. Take some time to turn your dream into a goal. Jot your notes on the following lines.

_____

_____

_____

_____

_____

4

UNEVEN CASH FLOW

*P*aying bills made Li crazy. Some months, if she had several gigs, she had more money than she needed. She loved to shop, and she spent that extra cash. Then, if there was less work the next month, she might run short. She knew she needed to save money, but the process was frustrating. She needed a plan she could follow.

It's hard enough to create a cash flow plan or a budget when you have a traditional salary. When you earn money in irregular intervals, it's even more difficult. And yet, to meet your goals, it's important that you find a way to organize your bills and your income.

Many jobs involve a structured salary schedule. Workers may get paid monthly, every two weeks, or weekly. It doesn't matter. They know when the next check is arriving. However, when you are a creative, that schedule can be unclear.

You might earn enough money, but you don't receive it regularly. The most significant danger here is spending too much money when it arrives and having a shortfall before the next check. This mistake is easy to make, but you can correct it. Remember how I asked you to track your spending in Chapter One? This calculation is the amount of money you must have available each month that you aren't receiving other income.

You might want to open a second bank account. One account holds the money you have earned, and then each month, you transfer the amount of your bills into the second account. That way, you can watch your funds dwindle, as traditional workers do, without seeing a larger sum you might be tempted to spend. Ideally, the money you have earned provides a surplus above your bills. We will talk about how to handle those extra funds later. Of course, you can have spending money, but be certain you're reserving enough cash to pay the bills until your next check.

One of the first issues you should understand is how often you will receive payments. As you begin your life as a creative, you will undoubtedly have another job that provides regular income. If you are at this point in your career, keep a journal of how often and how much money you have earned in your creative pursuits. As your career progresses, these numbers should improve, and the information will help you understand how many months in advance you should plan. I know you may be saying that if you just quit your job, you would earn enough to live with the additional time you would have. That might be true, and it might not.

I'm a professional worrier, and I know how hard it is to earn enough money as a creative to live. I want you to make pessimistic assumptions, not optimistic ones. This may be out of character for you. It's out of character for me. I am a believer in things that could happen. However, financial concerns will drain your creative spirit. Having money set aside will help you prosper.

Activity

Uneven cash flow is the pits. It's so easy to spend too much when you have plenty of money in the bank or your cash app. And yet, if you don't earn enough the next month, you may run short. Creating a cash flow statement is more important when your money is sporadic. That doesn't mean you can never buy anything; you just need to be careful how much you spend. You calculated your monthly bills in an earlier chapter. Use that information to help you decide how much you need to save when you have money. Jot your notes on the following lines.

5
EMERGENCY FUNDS

ow could everything she owned break at once, Lara wondered, as she stood by the shredded tire. Today, it was the car, but yesterday, her toilet wouldn't shut off, and the day before that, she had to replace the damper pedal on her keyboard. She had a credit card she could use, but she hated the interest she knew she would pay.

Emergency funds are a common component of financial planning. An emergency fund is a stash of cash available for income loss or expensive emergencies. The savings should be held somewhere accessible, in an account that shouldn't lose money. In other words, your emergency fund isn't an investment account like an IRA. I know it's tempting to count your investments toward your emergency fund, but the move is dangerous. The market can be in freefall when you most need access to the cash. Instead, put it in an FDIC-insured bank account. Most US banks have FDIC insurance, so you can usually choose the account with the highest yield (interest rate). If you are prone to spending your emergency fund, open an account in a different bank, don't put a debit card on the account, and don't link it electronically to your primary bank. That way, it is difficult to access the money.

Saving an emergency fund can be discouraging, especially if your finances are tight. Financial celebrities will tell you that you should have six months' worth of your bills saved. If you don't have any money in the bank, that amount seems impossible. Instead of focusing on a huge goal, I want you to break it into small pieces. Begin by trying to save a two-week emergency fund. Rather than multiplying your monthly bills by six, I want you to divide them by two. That number should be less intimidating. Begin to save toward that goal.

I talk to many people who believe they should save substantial money each month, but they find it impossible and quit. Then, they aren't saving any money at all. Saving small amounts regularly will get you to your goal. Maybe you can't save a couple hundred dollars a month, but you might be able to save twenty-five. That amount adds up. In a year, you've saved $300!

One way to find money to save is to try to save half of any extra cash you earn. Maybe you earn a larger-than-expected tip. Save half of it, and then you can spend the other half. If you win a contest, again, save half and do anything you want with the rest. People laugh at me when I say you should have spending money, but I see your financial success much like a weight loss program. You must live within your budget for the rest of your life. If I offer advice that's impossible or draconian, you won't take it. I want you to see the changes you're making now as permanent. To do that, you need spending money.

Of course, I don't think it's sufficient to have only two weeks of bills in savings. Once you are successful, I want you to do that repeatedly until you reach your savings goal. The COVID-19 pandemic changed how I view emergency funds. I never considered that entire industries could go away for months. Sometimes, primary jobs like acting or music disappeared, and secondary jobs like waiting tables or working retail vanished, too. COVID disproportionately hit the arts community. Because we can't know the future, I would like your ultimate goal to be saving six months of your bills. However, I want you to break it into small pieces and celebrate each win. Even if you don't have half a year of bills saved, you will eventually get to three or four months. That would have made a big difference in 2020, and I believe it would be a massive benefit for the next unexpected event. Hopefully, we have many years to learn whether or not I'm correct.

Activity

Life happens, and sometimes, it's expensive. If you don't have an emergency fund, start by choosing an amount you can save every month. Put it in a separate bank account, try not to link it to other accounts, and certainly don't add a debit card. If something goes wrong, you can use the money, but you have to put it back. Jot your notes on the following lines.

_____

_____

_____

_____

6

CREDIT

mi didn't know how it happened. One month, she couldn't quite pay off her credit card, and she just went downhill from there. Now, it had been two months, and she had little hope of ever paying off her debt and improving her credit score.

Our credit score impacts almost everything we try to do financially. Our credit score matters whether we want to buy a house or vehicle, borrow money, or even rent an apartment. Trying to acquire credit or improve your credit score can be frustrating. Fortunately, there are a few steps you can take.

Sometimes, I talk to people who don't have the credit score they anticipated. If you have paid off everything and don't use a credit card for anything, you may find yourself without credit after a few years. If you're just getting started and you've never borrowed money, you may not have a score, either.

Your bank may be a good place to start creating your credit score through a credit-builder loan, sometimes called a "fresh start" loan. In this program, you apply for a loan from the bank, but rather than being given the money right away, they keep it. You make regular, on-time payments, and when you have repaid the loan amount, they give you the money.

The advantage of a credit-builder loan is it shows your ability to make monthly payments. These are reported to the three credit bureaus: Equifax, Experian, and TransUnion. Your timely payments begin to create a credit score.

If you want a credit card, begin by applying for a gas card. These cards are sometimes less difficult to obtain, and buying gasoline is something you are doing anyway. Put your gasoline payments on the card, lay back the cash each time, and pay the balance in full monthly.

Regular payments where you pay off the card will help you build your credit score. Additionally, you are less likely to buy more than gas and an occasional fountain drink. It's hard to get into credit card debt at most gas stations.

Once you have established your credit, you will want to apply for a traditional credit card. Most people need at least one card, because they conduct transactions, like renting a car, where a card is required. Additionally, using credit regularly will help you obtain better loan rates for major purchases like homes or vehicles.

If you have credit card debt, you should try to pay it off. I'm never going to be judgmental because credit card debt can sneak up on you. Your goal is to figure out how it happened, get it paid off, and try to avoid it in the future.

People have many ideas about how to pay off credit cards. The best one financially is to pay off the highest interest rate first. Then, apply the payment from that card to the next payment until everything is paid off.

Sometimes, the amount of debt on the high-interest card can be overwhelming. If you would rather pay off smaller balances and tackle the large balance last, I'm not going to argue with you.

You need to figure out a system that works for you. If the small debts are making you crazy, pay them off. Then, apply all the money from those payments to the larger balance.

The worst thing you can do is not pay off the debt at all. Even worse, sometimes people add to it because there doesn't seem to be any hope. Don't fall into that trap. If you can't figure out how the debt is increasing, look at your purchases. What could you eliminate? Where could you substitute a less expensive alternative? I rarely stop to buy a coffee. I have travel cups and take my own from home or work.

If you don't want to give up your coffee, find something else you can eliminate. I also bring my lunch to work most of the time. I don't want to spend ten to twenty dollars a day eating, and I try to save eating out as a treat. I help myself by leaving things I like at the office. If I like it, I'll eat it. If I don't, I'll spend money to eat something else. I've learned what works for me, and I'd encourage you to do the same thing.

Once your credit score is good, keeping it that way will be more fun than building it. However, the process of building credit is critical for long-term financial success. Take small steps, follow through, and your score will get better before you know it.

Activity

Create a plan for building or improving your credit. A great place to start might be with a credit-builder loan from your bank. If you need to pay off bills, create a strategy you can sustain until you succeed. Jot some notes on the following lines.

7

SAVING FOR BIG EVENTS

hen Steve and his husband got married during COVID-19, money was tight. Neither was earning much from their art studio or their side hustles of driving for hire or waiting tables. It was tough. Now, they were both working again, and they wanted to take a honeymoon. They still had lingering fears about spending too much, so they wanted to plan their trip carefully,

People often have more joy in planning trips and events than remembering the event once it has passed. We love the anticipation that culminates in the happy occasion. I believe that one reason the memory of the event is less joyful is that it often comes with a large credit card bill.

I am not judgmental about people using credit cards. What does worry me is when people put items on the card without knowing how they will pay for them. Vacations are a frequent culprit, but so are the holiday season, other gift-giving events, and weddings.

With a little planning, you can avoid the sticker shock of big purchases. To begin, some of these events occur regularly. Many people give gifts during the holiday season and on birthdays. Most folks also take a vacation each summer. For recurring events, include them in your regular expense list we created earlier.

To get an accurate amount, look at your records and see what you spent. If you didn't keep records, then do it next time. Write down every dime you spent during the holidays. Include special food and booze. Then, take this amount and divide it by six. If you can't save that amount monthly on top of your other obligations, consider spending less.

Track all the expenses around your travel. Most people travel during the summer, so after the holidays, you have about six months to save for your vacation. Again, you might want to rethink your costs if you can't save the amount during six months. If you can have the money saved before the event, the post-event lag won't be as difficult.

It's so easy to spend more than we intended. As fun as the holidays appear, they can be quite stressful. Many people get caught in the trap of not wanting to disappoint those they love, often their children, so they compensate with extravagant gifts. Again, no judgment, but don't try to offset missing a recital or your need to work long hours by purchasing expensive items. You can create great memories with your children that aren't expensive.

During the holidays, you can drive around and look at the festive lights. Take a thermos of hot chocolate to avoid having to stop for drinks. To teach your children to be generous, volunteer at a community kitchen or some other place where they can give to the less fortunate. Make cookies, even if they are "slice and bake."

On vacation, buy the ingredients for a picnic. You don't need a charcuterie board. Make sandwiches and buy bottles of your favorite beverage. Then, find a beautiful location. If you aren't going on a trip, drive to a local park. Play games, splash in a lake, and then search for fireflies if you can still find them! Look for other creative ways to save money in all areas of your life.

Other purchases happen less often. It's easy to view items like luxury trips or weddings as once-in-a-lifetime events. We think the money is worth it because we won't do this again. Wedding planners and cruise ships tend to encourage this thinking. However, spending huge sums of money won't necessarily make the event better.

For these occasions, you want to estimate the expense and divide it by the number of months until the big day. If you can't comfortably afford to pay that much, look for ways of cutting costs. I promise you won't miss the expensive details later.

I said in an earlier chapter that cash flow is everything. Saving for annual costs or bigger events comes down to organizing your spending. The trick is to control expenses and start saving early. That way, your memories can be as much fun as the planning!

Activity

Big purchases often involve exciting times, whether it's a trip, a car, or a new musical instrument. Holidays and vacations can make life fun. However, saving significant amounts of money can be tricky. Follow the suggestions in this chapter, and jot your notes on the following lines.

_____

_____

8

WHY WE DO WHAT WE DO

Elise had grown up with a single mother who struggled financially. She heard her talk with frustration about how people with money didn't understand average people. Elise had been fortunate in her career. She was a college professor in the school of music, taught private violin, and played first chair in the community orchestra. She earned more money than her mother ever had, but she felt like sometimes she sabotaged her finances with poor decisions.

Making good financial decisions would be so much easier if we were logical robots. If we looked at our money options and made only good choices, we would all be financially ahead. Unfortunately, we're human, and most of us don't behave that way.

Some financial thought called "modern portfolio theory" is based on the concept of the "rational investor," the person who looks at all the information and always makes the correct choice that minimizes risk and maximizes return. Unfortunately for the analysts who follow this assumption, I've seen articles that list more than ten common situations where investors are not rational.

In fact, exceptions to modern portfolio theory are wide-ranging. Many people believe that the general concept isn't accurate enough to be taken on its own to guide investment decision-making.

Two areas of study, behavioral finance and interior finance, attempt to explain how and when people do not make rational investing decisions. Behavioral finance looks at broad, cultural, and macro reasons why we make financial errors. Interior finance, on the other hand, looks at the relationships with our family, friends, and social networks, the micro reasons why we make financial mistakes.

For example, herding behavior bias, or the desire to follow the crowd, is a behavioral finance concept that provides one reason why we have market bubbles and why they burst. Additionally, familiarity bias leads us to believe that because we think we know something, that makes it true. This bias explains why people buy single stocks of companies they like without looking at their financials or business ratios.

For the sake of this chapter, however, I am more interested in discussing the thinking behind interior finance. Interior finance claims that the money beliefs held by the people you value influence your actions around money. One topic within interior finance is "money scripts." Money scripts are statements about money that are so much a part of what you believe that you don't even see them as opinions.

We all have money scripts. Maybe our parents taught us that if we worked hard, we could get ahead. Maybe a spiritual leader said that wealthy people should give back to those with less. Maybe we even heard that people who cared about money were greedy.

I believe that money scripts are a powerful influence on creatives. As I was trying to decide whether to write this book, I repeatedly read statements claiming creatives weren't good with money. I also read financial books written for creatives that said it directly or that the creative should just take the advice in the book and not worry about it.

I don't know about you, but I hate to be patted on the head and dismissed. I think you can be creative and love finances, be neutral, or hate them.

The activity at the end of this chapter may take longer than a week. You may have two or three immediate responses to your beliefs about money, but more may come to you over time. I want you to concentrate on the "why" of your belief. For example, I know people, both creatives and not, who tell me they hate money. Hating money makes it harder to be financially stable. It also makes being prosperous almost impossible, because they are acting against what they think is true and good. Before you can change beliefs, you must address the "why." Why hate money? Why can't you be good with money and be a creative? Only as you begin to answer these questions and more can you begin to change your relationship with your finances.

I'd like to offer a few other ideas that run against the stereotypes of creatives and money. First, being a starving artist isn't romantic. You can earn cash and not "sell out" your art. You can make a living by selling some of your pieces while you create others for pure joy. Finally, being wealthy doesn't make you a bad person.

What do you believe about money that's holding you back? Can you see flaws and create a way to live with new beliefs? I think everyone should prosper. Prosperity isn't all about your bank account, but without enough resources, it's hard to feel prosperous.

Activity

What are your earliest memories of money? What did your family believe? Your friends? Your faith community? Were the beliefs healthy or destructive, and how do you think they are impacting you today? Do other things, like relationships, impact your spending? Jot your notes on the following lines.

_____

_____

_____

_____

_____

9

FINANCIAL PROFESSIONALS

arter was amazed to learn that all financial professionals didn't have to put his best interest ahead of their own. After all, they could be holding all of his investments. When he discovered they might sell him specific products because they would make more money, he set out to learn more about the industry. He worried the most when his adviser ignored his concerns and told him to focus on his art and leave the financial decisions to the professionals.

As you go through the material in this book, you may decide you want some assistance. Working with the right financial planner can help you with both your investments and other planning issues, such as taxes, retirement savings, and insurance. A good financial planner is useful, while a bad one can cost you a lot of money. Given that risk, how do you know whom to select?

The most important characteristic of your financial planner is an enthusiasm to serve in a fiduciary capacity. This fiduciary standard is a legal obligation for a financial professional to act in the client's best interest. Of course, the professional will be paid, but the fees should be disclosed and reasonable. Additionally, the adviser's product decisions, like investments or insurance, should be made with the client's best interest first rather than the compensation. The fiduciary landscape has been changing regularly for the past few years, so let me review a few of the issues with you.

When I entered finance more than twenty years ago, I assumed that the people entrusted with your life savings would automatically act in your best interest. Unfortunately, that's not the law for many financial professionals. In fact, most have no fiduciary obligation to you. Even worse, in the financial services industry, some terms are now being used in ways that have potentially misleading definitions. For example, although the term "best interest" sounds like the advisers are fiduciaries, sometimes people using that term do not, in fact, have a fiduciary obligation.

To counteract this confusion, you should ask your financial professionals to hold a fiduciary standard. If they try to modify your request and won't commit to being a fiduciary in writing, consider a different adviser.

If you're wondering if you need a financial planner, remember they can help you organize your financial decisions in different parts of your life. Financial planners assist you with cash flow issues, saving an emergency fund, and paying off debt. They help you manage risk by explaining insurance products and their alternatives. Planners assist you with your investment portfolio, helping you find your risk tolerance level and create an asset allocation most suited to meet your financial goals. They can calculate how much money you need to save for retirement, explain your company retirement plan, and introduce other retirement savings vehicle options, like IRAs.

Additionally, planners look at your tax situation and help find ways to reduce your tax liability. They can provide an overview of your estate issues. If they aren't an attorney, they should encourage you to seek one's advice. Finally, financial planners provide guidance with other types of financial concerns, including paying for college and buying or leasing a vehicle.

As you try to decide whom to select to help you with your money, you will want to look at credentials. There are many kinds of designations a financial adviser can earn, and your potential adviser might have many sets of letters after his or her name. Pay attention to them rather than simply being impressed. Ask the focus of each acronym and what the adviser had to complete to earn it. Some courses of study are rigorous, while others aren't. You need to know the difference.

I'm a fan of the CERTIFIED FINANCIAL PLANNER™ (CFP®) designation. If you read the disclaimers at the beginning of this book, you will see that any time I refer to a "financial planner," I'm referring to a CERTIFIED FINAN-CIAL PLANNER™ practitioner.

The CFP® designation requires a six-hour closed book exam following a full year of coursework. Twenty hours of Continuing Education must be earned every two years, including an Ethics course. Additionally, CFP® pros have at least a bachelor's degree (in any program of study) and three or more years of experience in financial planning. They also agree to embrace that all-important fiduciary duty. The CFP® designation really is the gold standard for financial planners.

Of course, if you don't want financial planning, you may want your adviser to have a different designation. My belief is that you should work with the best person you can find and whose model is appropriate to your needs. It's reasonable to expect them to have additional education beyond their licenses. After all, you're trusting them with a lot.

After reviewing both their willingness to be a fiduciary

and what services they offer, there are a few more things for you to consider. Although designations and training are important, your adviser should also treat you with respect. Creatives often believe they aren't good with money, and many in financial services are happy to exploit that.

Further, if you don't pay attention, bad actors can earn more money by positioning you in things that make them the most profit. You don't need to become a financial expert. That's why you're hiring someone. However, as you go into a meeting with your adviser, a little knowledge is helpful. It gives you confidence and allows you to ask better questions. Reading this book is a good first step.

Activity

Be sure you and your financial adviser have the same expectations from the engagement. Know how much money he or she makes from services or recommendations. Verify a commitment to the fiduciary standard. Finally, look at designations. If you want financial planning and investment help, you likely want a CERTIFIED FINANCIAL PLANNER™ practitioner. Jot your notes on the following lines.

_____

_____

_____

_____

INSURANCE CHAPTERS

LIFE INSURANCE

ngela was a graphic artist and a high school art teacher. Her husband was the band director at the same school, and he also gave private lessons. Together, they made decent money. They weren't wealthy, but they were comfortable. However, if something happened to either of them, the other would have trouble paying the bills, let alone have the money to raise their two-year-old daughter. The insurance agent they met with told them they each needed a million-dollar whole-life policy. That seemed like a lot to Angela, but she had no idea. She decided to call a financial planner before she made any purchases.

Many people think that financial planning is only investment recommendations and life insurance sales. Although planning is more than these two items, adequate life insurance is critical for the prosperity of the people you love when, not if, you die.

Folks are sometimes leery about purchasing insurance, because they don't know how much they need. Salespeople can appear pushy, especially when they make broad statements like, "You need a million dollars of life insurance," without explaining why.

If you want to purchase a million-dollar policy, your loved ones will probably have financial stability. However, there is a way to narrow down how much life insurance you should buy. The process is similar to calculating your retirement need, a process we'll discuss later. However, your insurance needs require additional steps.

Both formulas require that you look at expenses that will be incurred in the future. However, to determine how much life insurance you need, you must calculate your need during different parts of your life, not just during retirement.

Insurance proceeds are often invested; however, the risk tolerance for your retirement and your life insurance may be different. Your beneficiaries may want to be more conservative with this money. As a result, your risk tolerance level may be lower. Maybe that decision isn't purely rational, but we've already talked about the lack of "rational investors." Additionally, no one is rational after someone they love has died. Your insurance need calculation should assume a very modest rate of return. Let's look at some other issues you need to consider.

Dying is expensive. Your final expenses will need to be paid quickly. Calculate how much this will cost.

Can your loved ones pay the bills on only their salary? Although your minor children will receive a modest Social Security benefit, kids are expensive. They likely need more money than they will be receiving. They will have all their normal activities, and your surviving partner may also need to pay for additional childcare. You can calculate this need by using a cash flow calculator. You would enter the annual financial need, the number of years you will need it, and a conservative rate of return. It might be easier to work with a financial planner because you aren't done yet.

Once you have calculated your surviving spouse's financial need along with the cost of the young children, you look at the next part of life. Once your children are out of high school, do you want to help pay for higher education? Again, your variables involve the years until they reach college age, the inflated annual cost, and a very conservative rate of return.

Once the children are grown, your partner may want to defer tapping retirement resources. Spouses have more options to do this than partners, so check the current IRS tax code. If retirement resources are used while your partner is younger, he or she may have a retirement deficit. Calculate the shortfall while your loved ones are still working age.

The final deficit is calculating any shortfalls while your partner is in retirement. Often, this is the easiest deficit to fill because of your additional retirement funds, added to theirs. That's why preserving this money becomes important.

All these needs are added together, and the total is the amount of life insurance you need to purchase. Maybe the amount is higher or lower than you expected, but you can have confidence you are purchasing the correct amount using the best information you have.

As you review each segment of your financial life, you may discover that at some point in your family's life, they don't have a deficit. For example, they may have a shortfall until your partner reaches retirement age. At that point, access to your retirement accounts may provide enough money to live comfortably.

When insurance needs come to a definitive end, then the purchase of term life insurance may be sufficient. Term life exists, as the name suggests, for a specific period of time. Be careful with your assumptions, however, as repurchasing term insurance after it expires can be expensive or potentially impossible because of underwriting limitations.

Whole life insurance, on the other hand, is in effect for your entire life. It is initially more expensive, but it avoids discovering your term insurance has expired, and you still have an insurance need you didn't anticipate.

Other types of insurance exist, but these two types of policies are the most common. Remember that the CFP® Board of Standards believes that insurance is purchased to provide cash to help the people you love when you die. Insurance is not designed as an investment vehicle because the account may be in decline at exactly the time you need it.

One final warning—you may have heard the axiom, "Buy term and invest the difference." Most of the time, this suggestion works in theory. However, in practice, I've found that people don't invest the difference. Instead, they spend the difference. If you want to pursue this strategy, confirm the difference in the price of the policies. Then, be sure you are laying aside that much money a month into a savings or investment account.

Other times, people buy term life because they cannot afford to buy whole life. If you are in that position, purchase term life insurance to cover your insurance needs. However, regularly reassess your insurance needs and cash flow. You want to be sure you have the coverage you need.

Activity

As you try to decide how much life insurance you need, look at your current expenses and the financial situation that would occur if your income were gone. Then, project this need forward. What needs will occur in the future? This information will help your financial professional determine how much and what kind of insurance you need. Maybe you need a million dollars, maybe less, or maybe more. Jot your notes on the following lines.

_____

_____

_____

_____

_____

_____

_____

_____

HEALTH INSURANCE

arrie had just turned twenty-six. Her mom had included her daughter on her insurance under the Affordable Care Act for as long as she could, but Carrie had aged out. She had a lot of bills, and she hated to pay for something else. She considered skipping the insurance purchase altogether; however, her mother said that wasn't wise. Carrie decided to go onto the ACA Marketplace to see if she could afford something.

In years past, one of the biggest obstacles to being a self-employed creative was the inability to get health insurance. Fortunately, since 2010, that problem has been greatly reduced through the passage of The Affordable Care Act (ACA), also known as Obamacare.

The ACA creates a Marketplace where anyone, regardless of any pre-existing conditions, can apply for and receive health insurance. The amount of premium you pay is not dependent on your health. Instead, it is only based on your income and if you are a smoker.

To qualify for the Marketplace, you must earn more than 150% of the federal poverty level. If you are single, in 2025, that amount is $15,060, and if you are married (not in a partnership), it increases to $20,440. If you earn less than that, you should qualify for Medicaid under the Medicaid expansion program, which we will talk about later in this chapter.

You can receive reduced premiums if you qualify for subsidies. You may be able to save some money, especially if your state pays lower wages. To receive a subsidy in 2025, you must earn less than $60,240 if you are single and less than $81,760 if you are married. If you have children, the maximum income level would be higher, with a family of four able to earn up to $124,800 and still receive a subsidy.

You can enroll in the Affordable Care Act late in the calendar year for the next year. Because the dates aren't constant, you will want to check the site for updates. Additionally, you can change or enroll in the ACA if you have a change in status. Maybe you lose your job, move from full-time to part-time, or become a seasonal worker. Maybe you get married, get divorced, or have a child. These situations change the details of your ACA coverage, and you will want to report them as soon as you can. In these situations, you don't need to wait until the end of the year to apply for coverage. The details can be found on www.healthcare.gov. Keep up with the current information, as the rules occasionally change.

The Affordable Care Act also makes it easier for young adults to keep coverage. The law requires that companies must provide coverage for adult children until they are twenty-six. They don't need to live at home, be a minor, or be a deduction on their parents' tax return. Even though young adults often don't have serious medical conditions, car accidents or unexpected illnesses can be catastrophic. Maintaining medical insurance is important for everyone.

Remember that the income level from ACA doesn't need to be earned from one job, like money you earn from your creative endeavors. It's all the income you earn over the course of the year. If you have another job to help pay the bills, that income also counts towards ACA eligibility or qualifying for subsidies.

If you don't earn enough to qualify for ACA coverage and you can't get coverage through your spouse or parent, then Medicaid expansion can provide health insurance benefits. Unfortunately, a number of states opted not to implement health care coverage through Medicaid expansion. Living in one of those states may catch you in a crack.

If you find yourself earning too little to qualify for the ACA and too much for Medicaid, look at the professional organizations of your creative endeavor. Many groups offer benefits for members, especially if they serve groups that have trouble obtaining coverage in other ways. It might be worth the dues to join and find a policy. Remember that no insurance can take your pre-existing medical conditions into account.

I know that navigating health insurance can be complicated. The government's website is very helpful, and there are agents in every state who can help you enroll in it if you don't want to complete it yourself online. Those agents may offer other options, as well. Be certain anyone assisting you is acting in your best interest. If you don't like the agent, enroll yourself or ask a family member or friend for assistance. Medical costs quickly become more than you can pay.

Activity

Everyone needs health insurance. I know it's expensive, but the Affordable Care Act has taken steps to help you pay for coverage. Go onto the site https://www.healthcare.gov/ and look at your options. Alternatively, find an insurance agent who will show you your ACA options. If he or she also shows other choices, look at them, too, if you like. Read the fine print. Jot your notes on the following lines.

_____

_____

_____

_____

_____

_____

_____

_____

_____

_____

DISABILITY INSURANCE

asha was relieved that her accident hadn't been worse. When she realized how close she came to dying, she shuddered. Still, she looked at the cast on her arm and hoped it would heal well enough to allow her to continue playing the violin in the orchestra. She was glad she had listened to her financial planner and purchased disability insurance.

Although most people realize the value of life insurance, they are more likely to be temporarily or permanently unable to work during their careers than they are to die. And yet, disability insurance is often ignored as people engage in financial planning. However, they would be in a serious financial crisis if they lost their paycheck.

Disability insurance comes in two forms—short-term and long-term. Typically, employers include short-term disability coverage in a cafeteria plan, also called a fringe-benefit plan, while long-term disability is usually purchased privately. Although you are more likely to use a short-term policy because you will probably recover fairly quickly, long-term coverage helps avoid financial disaster if you become permanently disabled.

The tax treatment of your benefit, should you need it, depends on who pays the premium. When you pay the premiums yourself on a disability policy, the benefit is not subject to income tax. However, if your employer pays the premium, the benefit is taxable.

Since disability benefits usually only replace sixty percent of the money you were earning, you don't want to lose any more to taxes. Once you lose a quarter or so of sixty percent of your salary, you may not have enough money to live.

If you are a self-employed creative and purchase disability insurance, assuming you pay for it in after-tax dollars, then you don't pay taxes on any benefits you receive. That's the advantage. However, because it is usually priced for groups, short-term disability insurance can be expensive to carry on yourself. Long-term disability is more affordable, mostly because it is less likely to occur. You can increase your emergency fund to cover those bills. Alternatively, see if any of your professional organizations offer benefits. You may be able to purchase a group policy.

Disability policies pay a benefit based on the amount you earn. When you don't have a traditional paycheck to prove your income, you will probably have to provide your filed tax return when you apply for coverage. In fact, you may even have to show two years of taxes. This information will help you obtain as much coverage as possible.

The kinds of disability benefits you can receive focus on how much work you can still do. The three categories of policies are informally called "own occ," "modified occ," and "any occ."

"Own occ," or own occupation, is likely the type of coverage you will need to get. With own occupation disability, being unable to do exactly what you do today qualifies you for coverage. If you are a painter or a musician, your coverage takes effect if you cannot paint or play music.

The next category, "modified occ" or modified occupation, pays when you cannot do your direct job or a related job. For example, if you are a musician and can no longer perform at the level you need and you can still teach music, your modified occupation coverage may not pay. You will need to consider your options before you decide how to handle this discrepancy. If you could be happy doing something career-adjacent, modified occupation insurance would save you money in premiums, but you need to decide if you could live in that world.

The final categorization is "any occ" or "any occupation" disability insurance. This type of disability only pays if you cannot work in any occupation. For example, assume you are a musical virtuoso, best-selling writer, Broadway actor, or any other position that is the pinnacle of your genre. You likely have a nice lifestyle that accompanies this endeavor. Because any occupation coverage only pays if you can do absolutely nothing, the results could be catastrophic. If you could be a greeter or fast-food worker, your insurance will not pay. Your insurance also doesn't care about your current income level and the crisis that a huge salary cut would have on you or your family.

Social Security disability coverage is any occupation coverage. It's hard to qualify, and if you eventually crack the code, the payment is low. You probably want to own coverage that will also help keep you in your home and driving your car.

Disability insurance is often ignored, but not having it can be devastating for you and the people you love. Talk to an insurance agent who works with other creatives, as they will be most able to help you find the policy you need and can afford. Being unable to create and unable to pay your bills is a stress you never need.

Activity

Sometimes, it feels like everyone wants you to purchase something else. I know money may be tight if you add another insurance policy premium, but if you were disabled, could you financially survive? Most of us can't. For creatives who must be able to dance, act, paint, sculpt, play an instrument, or complete another activity, becoming physically disabled can be catastrophic. Even a short time away from work can lead to financial pain. Disability insurance can help with this. Jot your notes on the following lines.

_____

_____

_____

_____

_____

_____

HOMEOWNER'S INSURANCE RIDERS

ea didn't own many expensive things before she bought her violin. She had renter's insurance, but after talking with her friends, she was pretty sure it wouldn't cover the instrument. She called her agent to ask about purchasing a rider that would add coverage of her violin to her traditional policy. Even though it was an extra expense, she couldn't afford to replace her instrument without it.

Most people maintain some form of homeowner's insurance. If you have a mortgage on your property, the loan company likely requires it. People who do not own their property often carry renter's insurance. There are many components involved in choosing property coverage, and I don't want to focus on them here. Instead, I want to talk about carrying the coverage you need specifically for your creative endeavor.

The first thing you should know is that traditional homeowner's policies offer limited coverage for some expensive items. The policy will pay up to a certain amount and no higher unless you purchase a rider. Riders provide additional coverage for items otherwise limited by the policy. For example, if you have expensive supplies, equipment, or instruments, you may need to purchase a rider. Talk to your agent and explain what you own. Take pictures of the item and find your appraisal information. You will need to provide this to the agent and may need it again if you make a claim.

A bigger problem can occur if your creative endeavor is a business. Business activities are usually excluded from personal policies. This means that items used in your business, like what we discussed above, may not be covered by your personal homeowner's or renter's policy. If something is stolen, destroyed by a fire, or lost in another way, your personal policy may not pay.

Do not try to hide your business activities from your insurer, and hope for the best. If you need to make a claim, you don't want to discover that you have no coverage. Talk to your agent about your business and look at your options. You may need to purchase a separate policy.

Additionally, any liability coverage you have through your property insurance may not extend to business activities. Even umbrella policies that provide additional coverage can be problematic. In a world where people find creative ways to hurt themselves, you don't want to be subject to a lawsuit.

If you go to an event, like an art festival, you may need to purchase additional property and liability insurance for the time you are displaying there. Talk to the coordinator about how to obtain coverage.

Finally, earth movement and natural flooding are not automatically covered by most personal or business policies. If you are in an area prone to landslides, earthquakes, or flooding, you will want to get riders or separate policies to cover these events.

Insuring the elements of your creative venture will allow

you to continue your work if the unthinkable happens. Even when money is tight, having the proper coverage can prevent a disaster.

Activity

Think about the risks that occur within your creative endeavor. Do you have property or a building that needs coverage? Do you have supplies, equipment, or instruments? Do you need coverage as you transport items to shows? Do you need coverage for other creatives who share your space? What activities could lead to your liability? Take some time to think of the answers to these questions, so you cover all your risks.

Talk to your insurance agent. If your agent isn't helpful, get recommendations from other creatives in your discipline. Jot your ideas on the following lines.

_____

_____

_____

_____

_____

INVESTMENT CHAPTERS

14

PUTTING TOGETHER
PORTFOLIOS

*C*hloe loved her job in graphic design. She made money being creative and got a paycheck every two weeks. *Unfortunately, her employer didn't offer a retirement plan, so she and her colleagues were on their own. They talked about investments occasionally, and some bought cryptocurrencies or speculative stocks. Chloe didn't think that made sense. She wanted to put together a more conventional portfolio. She didn't mind normal risk, but she didn't want to turn her portfolio into a trip to Las Vegas. She had no idea how to put together a reasonable collection of investment products.*

Most people aren't in the stock market because they think it's fun. Instead, they purchase investments to help them fund specific goals, often retirement and their children's education. Once they know how much they need to save and their risk tolerance, they create an asset allocation to help them achieve their goals.

Your asset allocation reflects how you divide your money between types of investments. These categories of investments are called asset classes. Asset classes can break into very large categories or more refined ones. The two largest

63

asset classes are equities (commonly stocks) and fixed income (usually bonds). Most people make their first portfolio decisions by deciding the percentage of equities and fixed income in their portfolio. The accepted assumption is the more equities you own, the riskier your asset allocation. We will talk more about risk tolerance in the next chapter. Additionally, many people purchase mutual funds or exchange-traded funds for their holdings in the different asset classes.

Asset classes rapidly become more specific than simply the major categories of equities or fixed income. For example, you can be more specific and select among many types of equities. One common equity asset class consists of large-cap companies in the United States. "Cap" stands for capitalization, which means size. A common US large-cap mutual fund tracks the S&P 500, the 500 largest companies in the United States. Other asset classes include mid cap, middle-sized companies and small cap, smaller but still publicly traded companies. International investments are another large asset class.

Equity asset classes can be even more specific by choosing a sector (like healthcare or technology) or a global region (like Europe, Emerging Asia, or even a specific country).

People often spend more time selecting equity asset classes than they do choosing fixed-income asset classes, but it's worth taking a look at the bond side, as well. Fixed-income asset classes include government and corporate bonds. From there, you can drill down into Treasuries, government agencies, investment-grade corporate, and high-yield corporate bonds. You can become even more specific by looking at different government and corporate bonds from developed countries or emerging international markets.

Different asset classes provide diversification to your investment portfolios. Although the entire stock market can drop at the same time, it's more likely that some asset classes will go down more than others. Additionally, equities might go down, while fixed income stays the same, goes up, or drops by less. Because you can't know the future, diversifying your portfolios is a good way to try to lower your market risk.

A few other asset classes should be mentioned because they can also provide diversification. Real estate and commodities (often focused on oil and gold) can respond to market conditions differently.

Although many people like the idea of selecting individual stocks, purchasing funds is safer than buying a stock because of the diversification offered by the fund. If you only purchase one stock and something goes wrong inside the company, you will suffer major losses. Although funds go down, they nearly always recover over time. However, if you still want to purchase single stocks, large companies will likely be safer, and then you can fill the other asset classes by using funds.

I would be remiss if I didn't mention cryptocurrency. I don't know the future of crypto, but right now, there is no clear leader among your many cryptocurrency options. Additionally, I do not believe the United States dollar is going anywhere. If you want to invest in crypto as a speculative move, proceed with even more caution than any single stock. Additionally, only purchase a small amount and leave the rest of your investments in less volatile holdings.

And finally, be careful of any investment that does not trade publicly on the stock market. Private investments might look appealing, but they have many risks. I believe the biggest risk is your inability to sell them if something goes wrong. Private investments in real estate took a shellacking during the 2008 housing bubble. Some people are still waiting for those real estate investment trusts to go public. Their money has been tied up for sixteen years! Additionally, to purchase these types of investments legally, you must meet certain net worth and experience criteria. Unfortunately, some advisers ignore this requirement. Publicly traded investments can go under, but even a crisis can be easier to manage if you have a public market for the security.

You have many choices when you are creating the asset allocation for your investment portfolio. Equities (stocks or stock funds), fixed income (bonds or bond funds), real estate, commodities, and cash or cash equivalents are the most common investments and the easiest to obtain on the public market. Unless you enjoy following the stock market, you may want to seek the help of a financial professional who is a fiduciary to help you make your final decisions. Putting together the right asset allocation is critical for investing success.

Activity

A financial planner can help you create an investment portfolio and even manage your holdings for you, but you can also do it yourself. Take a risk tolerance quiz. Does the answer reflect what you believe about yourself? Then, put together a combination of funds that reflect that level of risk. Remember that the more aggressive you are, the more you probably want to own stock funds, and the more conservative you are, the more you probably want bond funds, cash equivalents, or other safer investments. Jot your ideas on the following lines.

_____

_____

_____

_____

_____

_____

_____

_____

RISK TOLERANCE

hen Juan opened his investment account, his financial adviser asked him a few questions. When did he want to retire? Juan didn't know. He was thirty. How much did he worry about his investments? Not at all. He had never had an account before. He told the financial adviser he wanted to make money, and the adviser said something about being aggressive. Juan realized the adviser didn't seem to know that although he wanted a positive return, he was terrified about losing his investment.

You've taken the plunge and opened an investment account. Good for you! Or maybe you've had one for a while, but you aren't sure what to do with it. What mix of investments should you own? Remember, whether you participate in your company's retirement plan or open an Individual Retirement Account (IRA), you may be the one to choose how your money is invested. Even if you work with planners or advisers, they will ask you questions to help you decide what kind of portfolio is best for you.

We talked about different kinds of investments in the last chapter. Remember, stock funds are engines of growth, while bond funds offer diversification, provide income, and might lower risk. Other kinds of funds, like commodities or real estate, diversify even more.

How do you choose which funds to buy? The first consideration is your risk tolerance level. Generally, your risk tolerance is identified through your answers to a questionnaire. After you complete it, you are assigned a category based on your answers. These categories correspond to different levels of risk, from conservative to aggressive.

Of course, knowing you are moderately aggressive isn't that useful if you don't know how to put together a moderately aggressive portfolio! Fortunately, you often don't make these decisions alone. Your financial professional, employer, or the organization that created the questionnaire may recommend choices corresponding to your risk tolerance level.

Although I can't give you customized advice in this book, a conservative portfolio is often about eighty percent fixed income and twenty percent equities, while an aggressive portfolio could be ninety percent or ninety-five percent equities. A moderate portfolio is fifty percent/fifty percent or maybe even sixty percent equities and forty percent fixed income. These percentages can give you at least a basic sense of how to make your broadest asset class division.

Your risk tolerance is important. If you panic about your investment portfolio and sell during a market downturn, the results can be catastrophic to your long-term investing success.

If you sell at the bottom, and the market starts recovering, when do you start buying again? Sometimes, you may wait until you feel safe, and then the market might drop again. You don't want to get into the trap of buying high and selling low. That's a great way to continually lose money. You need to invest in a way that allows you to stay invested in good economic times and in bad.

However, there is a second component to creating your portfolio allocation you can't ignore. Some financial publications call this "risk capacity," but I think that term is confusing and vague. I call risk capacity the likelihood you can meet your goals at your desired level of risk. Or even more simply, are your investments going to earn enough money if you invest them in the way you wish?

Over the last twenty years, I have learned to put investment portfolios into the context of client goals. Unless you are a wealthy, famous creative, you aren't likely invested in the stock market because you think it's fun. Instead, you invest to help fund your retirement, pay for your kids' college, or some other expensive goal. Those goals have costs associated with them. In earlier chapters, I talk about how to calculate your financial need for retirement and life insurance.

Remember, as part of these calculations, we assumed a rate of return for your investment portfolio. Your projected return is related to your risk tolerance level. To give you some context, the long-term rate of return for stocks is eleven percent, and the long-term rate for bonds is five percent. On top of that, inflation will take a bite.

If you select "conservative" as your desired risk level, the portfolio may not grow enough to meet your goals. One of the greatest crises I've seen is when someone has reached retirement age only to find out they have been invested too conservatively for too long, and they don't have enough money.

You can take several steps to make sure this isn't your outcome, but you need to start as soon as possible. First, be sure that your actual portfolio returns line up with the assumed returns. You can research this yourself, but a financial planner would make the process easier. You will want to look at longer-term returns, because, in any given month or year, the market can be highly volatile. If your rate of return is higher than your needed rate, you likely don't have a problem.

If your projected rate is lower than your required rate, you need to take action. First, could you sleep at night if you raised your risk tolerance by one level? In other words, if you are conservative, could you live with moderately conservative?

Additionally, could you save a little more money every month? Extra contributions might make the difference between success and failure.

Finally, could you defer retirement? The best way to resolve an underfunded retirement is to wait a few years. You lower your need, and you increase your assets. Be sure to run your retirement projection again after your adjustments to be sure you're on track.

One final word about risk tolerance. Time plays a major role in the appropriateness of risk tolerance levels. The more time you have, the more time your portfolio has to recover from a downturn. Shorter time horizons often need more conservative investment/asset allocations.

Finally, I talked earlier about investing for goals. Your goals may have different time horizons, and, as a result, you might have multiple risk tolerance levels across different portfolios. If you have a college funding account for your teenager, you may want a more conservative allocation than you have for your retirement account.

Getting your risk tolerance level correct is critical for your investing success. Check your choices now, and then review them every few years to avoid unpleasant surprises. Planning today makes a big difference later.

Activity

As you complete your risk tolerance, balance your desire to make money with your concern about loss and your timeline to recover. Revisit your risk tolerance periodically and after any life change. If you have experienced trauma, like the death of a loved one or divorce, review your risk tolerance several times until you feel comfortable with your choice. Jot your ideas on the following lines.

16

COMPOUND INTEREST

etsy didn't like to talk about money. She didn't understand it, and she was sure she didn't have enough of it. Back in high school, a teacher told her if she invested money in her twenties, she would have a huge amount when she retired. At least at her current age of twenty-two, juggling three jobs so she could sing at night, it sounded like a huge amount to her. She couldn't imagine how an investment could grow to be so much. Before she tried to scrape together some funds, she wanted to understand the process better.

Albert Einstein called compound interest the most powerful force in the universe. What an amazing statement from perhaps the most influential physicist ever! However, his flattery doesn't help you understand the fundamentals of compound interest. Let's start by defining the term, and then you can see its power, too.

You can earn interest in two different ways: simple or compound. Simple interest is what is paid by bonds. If a $1,000 bond pays a five percent coupon, it gives you $50 a year of interest. Five percent of $1,000 is $50. At the end of the year, you still have a $1,000 bond and $50. By the end of the next year, you will still have your bond and yet another $50. This continues until the bond matures. At that time, you will receive $1,000 for the bond and your last $50 payment.

Compound interest is calculated differently. Compound interest is what your bank account earns. Let's assume the same parameters. You have $1,000 in your bank account, and the account pays five percent interest. At the end of the first year, just like with the simple interest bond, you have $1,050 in your account. But here's where the magic starts. By the end of the second year, you will have earned five percent interest on $1,050, giving you an ending balance of $1,102.50. You earned $2.50 more than if you earned simple interest for two years. If you continued this for ten years, you would have a balance of $1,500 in your simple interest account but $1,628.89 in your compounding account.

It's easy to access accounts that pay compound interest. As I said earlier, you earn compound interest from your bank, so your emergency fund will grow at a compounding rate. Of course, the bank may not pay as high as five percent, but the concept remains the same.

If you have an investment account, and you hold positions or replace them with other investments year over year, the growth from each year will compound the next year. So, if you earn eight percent in your investment account the first year, you begin the second year with 108 percent of the balance at the beginning of year one to grow at that year's return.

If you reinvest interest and dividends from investments, that increases the amount that can compound even more. If you choose to reinvest, you want to review your portfolio periodically with your financial planner to be sure that none of your positions grow so much that they throw your asset allocation out of alignment.

For example, assume you begin with a sixty percent equities (stock)/forty percent fixed income (bond) portfolio, and stocks grow at nine percent while bonds grow at four percent. Eventually, your sixty/forty portfolio will get out of balance. You have different options that have nothing to do with compounding interest, so I won't go into those in this chapter. However, you should create a plan with your financial professional.

Isn't compound interest cool? I think Einstein was right. Earning money on your money is magical, and compound interest can help you meet your financial goals.

Activity

Calculating the growth from compound interest without a calculator is difficult. However, you can find calculators online or use the formula function in Excel. You can even download a financial calculator app to your phone. If that sounds like too much work, see a financial planner. The more you understand the power of compound interest, the more rewarding you may find saving and investing money. Even small amounts can make a big difference over time. Jot your ideas on the following lines.

_____

_____

_____

_____

1 7

THE RULE OF 72

enry was in his early fifties, and although he had no desire to retire from the theater where he worked, he wondered how much his investments would be worth when he was seventy. He didn't want to bother his financial advisor, do complicated math, or buy a calculator. Was there an easier way?

When you're saving money for a long-term goal, the progress can seem frustrating. You know you want your money to grow, but it can be difficult to see success. I know a shortcut that will be helpful. A financial phenomenon, "The Rule of 72," lets you understand how long securities will take to double in value.

The best thing about "The Rule of 72" is you don't need a calculator, and you don't need to be good at math. All you need to do is multiply the number of years your money will be invested by its rate of return. When the product is 72, you will have doubled your investment.

Let's look at an example. If you invest a lump sum of money for nine years and earn an eight percent rate of return, your money will have doubled because 9 x 8 = 72. If you're more conservative and have a six percent rate of return goal, your money will take twelve years to double because 6 x 12 = 72.

This shortcut only works if you invest the money one time or have a single lump sum you're trying to project. If you're investing $100 a month for nine years, you will need to use a financial calculator or talk to a financial planner to help determine the final value.

Even with the lump-sum limitation, "The Rule of 72" can provide a quick confirmation that you are saving enough for retirement. If you know how many years you have before you leave your job and how much money you need to have saved by then, you can confirm what rate of return you need.

Too often, people select a risk tolerance level without determining whether it provides enough return to meet their goals. I can't tell you how many times I've seen people make the mistake. Remember that the risk tolerance level you select will impact how much money you can expect to earn. A more aggressive risk tolerance level has the potential to earn more return, while a conservative one will earn less. You should choose the risk tolerance level that allows you to sleep at night, but you need to know its impact on your long-term goals, especially your retirement. You don't want to discover you haven't saved enough when you are sixty-five.

The Rule of 72 provides an easy way to see if your actual rate of return gets you to your goals. Don't forget that if you are working with multiple periods, your initial investment number will change. For example, if you have a $10,000 account earning nine percent, your money will double in eight years. If you are more than eight years from retirement, you will do the calculation again, but this time, your beginning balance is $20,000. At the end of that period, your account would be worth $40,000. If you're young, you can see the remarkable progress you can make. You can thank the compounding effect that we discussed in the last chapter for your success!

Activity

You can find the historical rates of return for your investments on free financial websites. One of the best is Morningstar. Just go to www.morningstar.com and type in the symbol of your investment. If you don't know the symbol, you can also type in the name. Then, you can find the historical return data. Choose the time period of the return that is long enough to include both up and down markets. Five or ten years will give you a more reliable average than one year or year-to-date. Then, take 72 and divide that amount by the number. That will let you know how many years your money will take to double. Jot your notes on the following lines.

_____

_____

_____

_____

_____

_____

READING YOUR INVESTMENT
STATEMENTS

*B**erta thought she had done a good job. She opened an IRA and deposited money several times a year. However, each month, when her portfolio statement arrived in her inbox, she was sure it was written in a foreign language. Because she didn't have a financial professional, she wasn't sure whom to ask about it.*

If you have an investment account, you probably get monthly or quarterly statements from the company. They used to be mailed, but now you probably receive an email with a link. If you're like most people, you don't open the email at all. Maybe you tried to look at your investment statement a few times, but you gave up in despair.

Portfolio statements can seem confusing and intimidating, but they contain critical information. Let's look at a few of the most important sections. Your statement may not be arranged exactly like I organized this chapter, but you should be able to locate what I'm explaining.

At the top of the first page of the statement, you should find a date range. Usually, it will be a one-month period, but sometimes the range might be a three-month quarter or even a year. You want to confirm you are looking at the latest information.

The gains or losses from the statement period should be located very close to the date range. Usually, you will have two columns—one for the changes that occurred during the statement period and one for the year to date. Both sets of information are interesting, but you need to know what you are analyzing. Your gains and losses section should also include any contributions, distributions, and fees added or deducted from the account.

Below the gains/losses, you should see a list of investments. Often, the first numbers are any cash or money market funds. Then, the statement lists the details about your holdings. Usually, the description includes the name of the holding or fund, its symbol, what you paid for it, and its performance. Your equity and fixed income positions will often be separated, but that's not a tremendously important part of your statement.

The holdings section matters because you want to know what you own. You also want to see how each of your investments is performing compared to your other holdings. Remember that the point of diversification is owning investments that perform well in different environments. Often, stock and bond funds do not perform alike.

Still, if something is drastically underperforming, you might want to review it with your financial professional. Additionally, if you are making your own investment decisions, you might want to do a little research, especially if you have chosen single stocks rather than funds. Funds provide better diversification and are less likely to perform far outside the market behavior of that period.

The next section of your statement probably shows dividends and interest paid on your individual holdings. This money rolls into the overall balances at the top of the first page, but it's still important to know which investments pay cash on a regular basis. If you're looking at a retirement account statement, that cash is not currently taxable. However, if you have opened an after-tax investment account, the dividends and interest will be included in your taxes as capital gains. Here's a planning tip: If you have both kinds of accounts, put the higher-paying funds into your retirement account. Focus on growth positions, which pay fewer dividends and interest, in your taxable account. This organization will lower your current tax liability.

The next part of the statement, "Activity," is the hardest to understand. Investment accounts can have complicated accounting because all cash must be converted to money market. This creates transactions that show cash deposits and conversion to money market. Of course, you should read your statement; however, you might want to talk to your financial professional if you're concerned with the activity section. It's unlikely the investment company made a mistake.

The last section of your statement is pages and pages of disclaimers. Yes, read them once, but after you have a basic idea, they probably don't need to take up much of your time.

All parts of a financial statement are important because it is a legal document about your investment holdings. However, looking at your gain/loss, holdings, and cash generated through dividends and interest will go a long way toward understanding the document.

If you don't want to do anything else, at least open the file and check your balance. I know that can be scary, especially if the market is dropping. However, things may not be as bad as you think. If you have created an asset allocation based on your risk tolerance, those decisions will help buffer turbulence. And our imaginations are often our biggest drivers of fear.

Activity

Make the commitment to look at your portfolio statement each time you receive a new one. At least see if your account has made a profit during that period of time. Then, look at the performance of each position. Review other sections as you need. Jot your ideas on the following lines.

RETIREMENT

19

CALCULATING RETIREMENT
NEED

*J*eff's wife was a sculptor. She wanted to work forever; however, Jeff did not want to work that long. He wanted to be free to attend her events or go fishing at the lake. His wife made enough money to cover her expenses and add supplemental income, but they couldn't live on it. He wanted to be sure that when he retired, they would have enough money. A financial adviser told him he needed to have a million dollars invested in the stock market. Jeff wouldn't have been so concerned if the broker had asked him any questions before he blurted out the number. Jeff wondered how much money he really needed.

The most common question people ask me is whether they are on track to be able to retire when they want. The two easiest ways to answer this question are by using a financial calculator built for retirement savings or hiring a financial planner. Either way, you will need to provide accurate information to give you the best chance at success. Any financial projection can be wrong, but you can help by doing some work before you run the numbers.

Although many financial calculators work well, you want to be sure you select one that allows you to change its assumptions so that they better match your financial situation. Of course, you need to give the financial planner the same information, although the planner may be in a better position to help you figure out some of the answers.

First, you need to decide when you want to retire. How many more years do you have to save money? Remember that if you want to retire before you are eligible for Social Security or Medicare, you will need to meet those financial needs out of your savings.

You should also review any default life expectancy. You may need to adjust the time horizon if longevity runs in your family. Perhaps counterintuitively, I don't recommend lowering your expectancy if your parents died young. Medical advances suggest we could all live well into our nineties. Additionally, you shouldn't assume the Social Security life expectancy used to calculate your required minimum distributions (RMDs). Many people far exceed this age, and you want to be sure you have enough money. I recommend that my clients assume a life expectancy of at least ninety. With medical advances, living to one hundred is more than possible.

Next, you need to know how much money you will need each month during retirement. The best way to get this answer is to look at your spending today. Remember when I told you cash flow was the key to everything? Nowhere is that truer than in your retirement planning.

Once you know how much you spend now, look at those expenses. What will fall off? What will be added? Will your house be paid for? Will you want to travel more? Estimate your spending as best as possible and avoid rules of thumb. I think it's risky to follow a common assumption that you will spend eighty percent of your current bills. Many people I've worked with spend as much in retirement as they did when they were working. There's nothing wrong with this, but you need to know as early as possible.

Include a reasonable inflation rate. The long-term average is about three percent. If your calculator defaults to this, you are probably fine with not changing it. The calculator or your planner will be able to take your spending today and figure out how much it will be in inflated dollars when you retire.

You will also need the current values of your investment accounts and how much you are contributing to them each year. The calculator should ask for both values. Additionally, a good calculator or planner will also ask you for your projected Social Security benefit amount and any other monthly checks you receive. These numbers are all necessary to help you see where you are in the process of funding your retirement income need.

The final assumption is one of the most important. What rate of return is the calculator assuming your investments will earn? To give you some benchmarks, a very aggressive portfolio of only stocks might provide eleven percent, the long-term average return for equities. A very conservative portfolio might only provide a four percent or five percent growth rate. Although five percent is the long-term average for fixed-income investments, until recently we have been in a low interest-rate environment. Borrowing money has been easier, but fixed-income yields have been well below average. Finally, if you have invested with a moderate risk tolerance level, you might be able to use an eight percent rate of return projection based on the long-term averages of the holdings. Using the correct rate of return for your retirement analysis is critical.

A final component of your rate of return is the impact of inflation. If you are earning eight percent, your actual rate of return during retirement won't be that high. If inflation is running at three percent, that comes off the return. Your real rate of return is five percent.

All these assumptions should be calculator inputs. If you're working with a financial planner, he or she should also be able to help you with these numbers. However, if these assumptions are not part of your conversation, you need to ask. Predicting the future is always difficult. You need data to make the task easier.

Activity

You will probably need to talk to a financial planner or use a financial calculator to figure out how much you will need for retirement. However, your first step is to gather the information. You need to know how much you are spending today, what your investment return is now and will be during retirement, and an inflation assumption. You also need to know when you want to retire and how long you think you will live. Give yourself a nice, long life expectancy so you won't run into an issue late in life. Jot your ideas on the following lines.

20

WHY RETIRE?

enna wanted to set up her easel at state parks and paint shorelines bathed in the last colorful light of the day. She wanted to go to regional art festivals. She also wanted to sleep until noon and work until two a.m. Unfortunately, her day job had interfered with most of her plans. But not anymore. Today was the last day at her job. She would miss her co-workers, but as she carried her box of pictures and coffee mugs to her minivan, she felt like a teenager again.

We've looked at the numbers of when you can retire. However, in this chapter, I'd like to talk about why you want to retire—what you are retiring to instead of what you are leaving.

For people with traditional jobs that have mandatory hours, limited vacations, and too many ZOOM meetings, retiring can feel like an escape. If you are a creative who has a day job like this, you may see retirement as the way you will be able to pursue your creative passions.

However, sometimes people believe they should retire because that's the way the world works. When they turn sixty-five or so, it's time to hang it up. I want you to be cautious about pursuing this decision.

We just discussed how to calculate the money necessary for retirement. Of course, if you don't have enough resources, then continuing to work becomes mandatory. However, I'm suggesting that even if you have adequate resources, you need to ask yourself why you are retiring.

When people tell me that they want to leave the workforce, after I congratulate them, I ask them why. Sometimes, the answers are easy and plentiful, and sometimes, they look at me with confused expressions on their face. They tell me their age, and I ask them again why they are retiring. The world has changed, and this is no longer your grandfather's retirement.

Back in 1935, when Social Security was created, white women had a life expectancy of sixty-five and white men had a life expectancy of sixty-one. Minority life expectancies were worse, with 55.2 for women and 51.3 for men. The arbitrary age of retirement, sixty-five, was longer than everyone's life expectancy except white women's, who, on average, died that year.

More recently, in 2021, white life expectancy was 77.5, and black life expectancy was 72.8. Of course, many people live much longer, and some live less—that's what an average means. However, Social Security was never intended to fund decades of income.

I'm not telling you not to retire; I just want you to ask yourself why you want to stop working. Remember that the easiest way to improve your retirement funding is by delaying your retirement a couple of years. Of course, you may hate your job, your health may be an issue, you may need to provide caregiving, or you may have big plans. All of these are valid reasons to retire.

However, if you're retiring only because you think you

should, consider extending your working career if you like your job.

If you still want to retire, I have an important question for you: I know what you are retiring from. What are you retiring to? In other words, what's your plan for what you will do during retirement?

If you are a part-time creative, then maybe you want to pursue your art more. If you want to retire from being a creative, then you need a plan for the rest of your life. Especially in the arts, stopping that activity can leave a large hole.

Retiring to something gives your life purpose. Gone are the days of sitting in a rocking chair on your front porch. Today's seniors look nothing like they did just a couple of generations ago. Do you want to travel? Spend time with family and friends? Get more involved in community or faith activities? The choice is yours, but you need to know what you're going to do before you quit your job.

On a more basic level, it's important to stay around people to avoid loneliness. Having meals together also ensures you eat real food, and it's fun. Stay active to avoid broken bones and physical degeneration. Stay mentally involved to stave off dementia.

When people retire without a plan, they often find themselves less happy than they expected. Life expectancy also drops when people don't have a purpose in life. If you want to spend more time on your creative endeavors, be sure to read the chapters in this book on running a business. The more time you spend working in your craft, the more you will want to ensure you make a profit and handle your taxes properly.

Retirement isn't an end; it's the beginning of a new chapter. Embrace the change, and your life will be much happier.

PEGGY DOVIAK

Activity

When we think about retirement, we often see it as a
destination. Take some time to dream about what your
retirement could be. Do you want to spend more time on
your creative pursuits? Do you want to travel? Do you want
to spend time with friends and family? The choices of your
next steps after retirement are yours. Jot your ideas on the
following lines.

_____

_____

_____

_____

_____

_____

_____

SOCIAL SECURITY

y day, Izumi worked in an accounting office, but a couple of nights a week and on the weekends, she also played acoustic guitar with a folk group. They were popular and usually had more gig offers than they could accept. They were all close to the same age and talked about retiring a little early to pursue their music. Izumi was sixty-two, and she knew she could take her Social Security benefits, but she didn't know if she could earn money, too.

Company pension plans used to be huge perks offered by employers. These plans required no investment decisions on the part of the participants. When the employees retired, they just received a check from the company every month.

However, most of us don't have pension plans at work anymore. The closest replacement we have is Social Security. Fortunately, Social Security is available for everyone, including creatives, as long as they have made the required contributions into the system. We will talk more about employment taxes later.

Your Social Security benefit is based on your highest thirty-five years of employment. Once you reach the maximum length, then higher-earning years can replace lower ones. This replacement creates a motivation for delaying retirement.

Remember that although you can take an early Social Security benefit when you are sixty-two, you will be penalized if you earn income over certain thresholds. In 2025, if you take Social Security before full retirement age and earn more than $23,400 a year, you will lose one dollar for every two of your benefits. Let's assume your Social Security payment at the age of sixty-two should be $1,000, and your full retirement age is sixty-seven. If you earn $30,000 when you are sixty-two and you claim your Social Security early, your benefit amount would drop to $500. The government doesn't keep the other $500. They put it back into your pot of benefits, and you receive the amount of the reduction spread over your lifetime.

Once you reach full retirement age, you can draw your benefits and earn as much as you want. You can also postpone taking Social Security until you reach the age of seventy. Every year that you defer your Social Security benefit between the ages of sixty-two and seventy, your benefit grows by eight percent. Eight percent is a respectable rate of return. Using long-term averages, it is what you could hope to earn from a moderate investment portfolio. If your finances are stable and your personal circumstances allow, you might consider postponing your benefit as long as possible.

Many people also are confused about their eligibility to receive their spouse's Social Security. There are several rules that govern how you could receive this benefit. First, you must be married for the rules to apply. Next, you are eligible to either receive your full benefit or half of your spouse's benefit, whichever is higher. You can't claim both benefits, and you can't receive all of your spouse's payment. Still, if your spouse earned significantly more money than you, you might receive a larger amount by claiming half of their Social Security benefit.

Today, the Social Security Administration rarely sends paper statements. Instead, you should register for an online account in one of two ways. One method involves completing a standard application, and the other offers enhanced security. Some of the enhanced questions are very difficult, and you may have trouble remembering detailed financial events from your past. You may have to create your account with the traditional level of security. Although anything can be hacked these days, I have a regular account.

Finally, although people are worried about the future of Social Security, I believe that the government will do whatever is necessary to continue making payments. If modifications do occur, I believe they would focus on younger workers and would not result in the end of the Social Security system. The uproar would be extraordinary, and politicians love to keep their jobs!

Activity

If you aren't paying into Social Security, download the forms, use software, or hire a bookkeeper to help you stay up to date. It's required by law, and the benefit you will receive during retirement will make years of bills easier to pay. Jot your notes on the following lines.

_____

_____

22

INDIVIDUAL RETIREMENT
ACCOUNTS

ria loved acting in community theater, and she adored being with her creative friends. However, she also worried about her finances and wanted to protect her future. She saw too many of her peers going year after year without saving money. They said their retirement plan was never to retire. She wanted to open an IRA, and she had heard of a Roth, but she didn't know very much about it.

Even when you love what you do, you might want to retire someday. And when you make your money in the arts, you often don't have an employer who offers a retirement plan. It's up to you to save for yourself. The easiest kind of retirement account to open is an Individual Retirement Account (IRA).

You may have heard of the two types of IRAs—traditional IRAs and Roth IRAs. Traditional IRAs are often funded in pretax dollars. The IRA grows without tax consequences until you remove money from the account. Those distributions are then taxed at your current income tax bracket. The thinking behind deferred taxation is if you are earning good money today, you may be in a lower tax bracket when you are in retirement because you are making less money. Potentially higher tax rates and spending levels beg the question of whether that assumption is true. However, if you want a tax deduction today, a traditional IRA can meet that need.

The other kind of IRA is a Roth. Roth IRAs are funded in after-tax dollars, and the distributions are free from income tax if you follow certain rules. First, for tax-free deductions, you must be 59 ½, and you must have opened a Roth at least five years earlier. Even if you have multiple Roths, the five-year period begins with the opening of the first account. Especially if you are early in your working career, you may be in a lower income tax bracket today than you will be in the future. If you pay your taxes and fund your Roth, you may save money.

The second advantage of a Roth is the ability to withdraw your contributions without a penalty. If you withdraw money from a traditional IRA before you are 59 ½, with a few exceptions, you pay a ten percent penalty on the distribution in addition to paying the tax due. However, you can withdraw your contributions to a Roth without tax consequences (since you already paid them) and without a ten percent penalty.

Let me give you an example. Assume you put $500 in a Roth, and your deposit grows by $100. Now, the account is worth $600. If you have an emergency and need $500, you can take it from the Roth with no taxes or penalties. You cannot take the $100 of growth before you are 59 ½ without incurring both taxes and penalties. Although treating your retirement savings like a revolving door has its own risks, many people are hesitant to lock up money for decades, especially if they are young.

In 2025, the contribution limit for both traditional and Roth IRAs is $7,000, with a $1,000 catch-up contribution possible if you are fifty or older. Remember, that's the total contribution. You can fund one kind of IRA or both kinds, but the total you can deposit is $7,000.

Additionally, if you earn over certain income levels, and have another retirement plan, you cannot deduct your contributions to your traditional IRA. For 2025, those limits are $87,000 if you are single or $143,000 if you are married and file jointly. The limit is the top end of a phaseout, so consult your tax professional for the details. Above these levels, you can fund the full amounts, but you cannot take that amount off your taxes. Further, if you are single and earn over $165,000, you cannot fund a Roth at all. If you are married, that income level increases to $246,000. Again, there are phaseouts, so be careful.

I realize that some higher-income creatives might be impacted by these limits; however, I often see another problem. Sometimes, finances are tight, and contributing to a retirement plan seems impossible.

The idea of putting aside $500 a month or more might seem unattainable. If so, I am not going to be critical, but don't let good be the enemy of great. If you could put $100 a month into your IRA, you may be pleasantly surprised with how much you will have saved in a few years. Will that pace of funding provide enough money for your retirement account? Probably not, but it's better than saving nothing at all. As your financial situation improves, your funding level can increase. When you can put aside more money than the contribution limits allow, you have additional options. We'll talk about those in the next chapter.

Activity

An IRA is a great way to begin to save for your retirement. Although a financial planner might make the process easier, you can open your own online account. If you need

the tax deduction today, you might want to open a traditional IRA. However, to save future taxes, you would want to
open a Roth if your income level allows. Jot your notes on
the following lines.

_____

_____

_____

_____

_____

_____

_____

_____

_____

23

SEPS AND SIMPLES

alaal was making enough money selling his pictures that he was able to fund his Roth IRA at the maximum level. He didn't know if it would provide enough savings for his retirement, and he wanted to put more money aside with some kind of tax advantage. He wasn't sure if he could create a 401(k) for himself. He wondered if he had more options.

As you become more successful in your creative endeavors, you may want to lay back additional money for retirement. Funding an IRA is a great first step, but you have further options. The two easiest retirement plans for self-employed individuals are SIMPLE IRAs and SEP IRAs. They are free to set up, require little administration, and are available if you don't have a separate business structure like an LLC or S Corporation.

SIMPLE IRAs provide you with the ability to fund your retirement at higher levels than allowed in traditional or Roth IRAs. In 2025, you can typically contribute $16,500, with an additional $3,500 if you are fifty or older. If you run your creative endeavor inside a business structure, you likely can contribute those amounts into your SIMPLE, assuming your income is high enough. If you are self-employed, you can also fund your account. However, you will need to deal with an additional wrinkle.

If you include the income from your creative endeavor on Schedule C on your personal taxes, you are self-employed. For any retirement plan employer contribution, you must reduce your income level by both half of the employment taxes you paid and all of your personal contribution to the retirement plan. Let's break that sentence down. When you earn money, you must pay employment taxes—Social Security and Medicare. Usually, you pay half, and your employer pays the other half. But when you are self-employed, you function as both employer and employee. As a result, half the amount of your employment taxes is deducted before you calculate your employer contribution. Additionally, your employer contribution amount is reduced by any money you, as the employee, contributed to the plan.

Wow, that's a mouthful! The result of these deductions calculates your net income from self-employment. The process sounds worse than the practice. Your best bet is to review IRS examples, or better still, talk to a CPA and see how they calculate the number. Then, you can basically copy what they did.

Opening the account is easier. To open a SIMPLE IRA, you complete Form 5305-SIMPLE. It may sound strange to think of yourself as both an employer and an employee, but you are. If you have any other paid employees, you will need to include them if they earn more than $5,000 a year from you.

However, you aren't under a large financial liability by including your employees. SIMPLE plans work a lot like 401(k)s. You can structure any money you give your employees to come in the form of a three percent match.

This means if your employee puts in three percent of his or her earnings, you must do the same thing. However, if they don't participate, you don't have any liability. If you want to put money into their plan whether they participate or not, you can give them two percent of their earnings. In this scenario, you can occasionally skip years if money is tight.

Most of you don't have employees. The same rules apply to you as you function as both the employer and employee. If you set up your plan to match contributions, if you (the artist) deposit three percent of your earnings, you (your employer) also deposit three percent, adjusted for self-employment income, as we discussed earlier. However, you can also personally contribute up to the maximum amount. Only three percent would be matched.

Even if you don't anticipate employees, I recommend opening the plan as a match. That frees you from having to deposit any money into the plan if finances are tight.

If the money from your creative endeavor is very stable and you want to increase your retirement deferment more than the SIMPLE allows, you could consider a SEP IRA. SEPs are also easy to open by completing a form 5305-SEP, and like the SIMPLE, there are no startup costs. SEPs allow the same level of deferment as a 401(k) plan, $70,000 or twenty-five percent of their compensation, whichever is less. The wrinkle to the SEP is that all the funding comes from the employer, and funding levels must be the same for all employees. This means if you wanted to make a twenty-five percent contribution for your own account, you would have to do that for any employee, as well. Additionally, the definition of employee for a SEP is generous. If someone has worked for you for three years of the past five and earned $750 in the last two years, you probably have to include them in the plan.

Of course, you want to take care of your employees, but

SEP contributions can put a strain on your cash flow. SEPs are usually better choices when you have no intention of hiring anyone.

Before you open either type of account, read the fine print. You might also want to check out IRS Publication 560 for more details. SIMPLEs and SEPs are great retirement savings vehicles, but you and your financial team need to consider your situation, especially if you are self-employed. I omitted 401(k) plans, because I think they are usually more complicated and expensive than most creatives need. However, if the SIMPLE or SEP don't work, you should consider all your options.

Activity

If you want to put more than the IRA limit into a retirement account, you might consider opening a SEP or a SIMPLE IRA. Look at the characteristics of each kind of account and choose the one that fits your business model the best. Jot your notes on the following lines.

_____

_____

_____

TAXES

24

HOBBY OR BUSINESS?

Everyone in Char's critique group viewed themselves as an author. However, not everyone thought they were professional writers. Char wanted to earn her living as a writer, and she saw it as a job. However, she knew that the IRS scrutinized people who claimed creative undertakings as a business. She wanted to take the steps necessary to win an audit should she experience one.

Are your creative endeavors a hobby or a business? Hobbies bring us joy and fulfillment. However, treating your efforts like a hobby creates different tax consequences than if you want your talent to be a career or side hustle. If your activities are part of a business, your losses can be greater than your gains, but if they're a hobby, you can only take losses up to the amount of income you earned.

Let's look at an example. Assume you are a painter, and your expenses for the year are $1,000, and your income is $100. If your painting is a business, you can take a $900 loss on your personal taxes. If your painting is a hobby, your $100 won't be taxable, but you can't take a deduction. As you can see, the classification matters.

Because of the potential deductions, the IRS has strict

rules about differentiating your work as a hobby or a business. I am going to summarize some of the more important requirements below, but you should review the link to a news release, other IRS material, and the opinions of your CPA. It's important to work with someone who has other creatives as clients, so the advice they give is accurate and not overly restricting or generous.

First, you must keep records and receipts of income and expenses. If you lose paper receipts, ask for them electronically or take pictures of them. Ideally, you would keep files, but at least put them all in the same drawer, so you can find them later.

Next, you must devote significant time to your activity, like you would for any other job. Keep records of the time you spend. You don't have to track your work by the minute, but the more specific your time recording is, the more your document will look like legitimate information. You can track daily in a day planner, or you can keep your information electronically. Some phone or computer apps are designed to help you focus. As part of the process, they track your time. These records could support your claims.

Further, the IRS wants you to depend on income from the activity for your livelihood. It also wants you to have income from other sources sufficient to cover any losses sustained by your creative endeavors. Keep records of how you use your artistic revenue and set an early goal of having enough to pay a specific bill.

Of course, normal startup losses are expected, but the IRS wants you to demonstrate that you are taking steps to move toward profitability. Taking classes or entering contests would be good ways of demonstrating these efforts. Again, keep your receipts and any critiques you receive. Additionally, increased marketing efforts would show good faith that you are trying to make money.

The IRS wants you to be profitable, at least some of the time, or show how you can expect to make a profit in the future. If you're struggling, keep excellent records showing that you are trying. If you don't, the risk of losing an audit substantially increases.

Finally, the IRS wants you to show that you have the knowledge you need to run a successful business. Purchasing this book is an excellent step! Keep your receipt.

Activity

The following IRS tax tip link provides a fairly comprehensive list of what the IRS considers as they decide whether your creative endeavor is a hobby or a business.

https://www.irs.gov/newsroom/heres-how-to-tell-the-difference-between-a-hobby-and-a-business-for-tax-purposes

If you consider your work a hobby, that's fine, but if you want business tax treatment, you will need to work regularly to keep that status. To help, you may want to consult a CPA or other tax professional who specializes in creatives.

_____

_____

_____

_____

2 5

DEDUCTIONS

*M*annie *always treated his dancing like a business. He tracked his income and expenses, and he paid his employment and income taxes. He and his friend went to New York for an audition. They weren't really expecting the parts, but it was a great excuse for a trip to the City. Mannie didn't deduct most of his costs, but his friend did. About a year later, his friend got a letter from the IRS asking to explain that portion of his tax return.*

In the next chapter, we'll talk about the home office deduction. However, in this chapter, I want to discuss other deductions you can and can't take and some pitfalls to worry about. I've categorized what I'm discussing, and the list is not exhaustive. Talk to a tax professional about your individual situation.

Taking a view from 50,000 feet, even if you are running your creative enterprise as a business, and the expenses are valid, you don't want to flood your tax return with thousands and thousands of dollars of expenses and very little income. Yes, you can run a business at a loss, but artistic endeavors can get the IRS' attention. Be cautious in what you claim.

Additionally, although you can deduct many expensive

purchases in the year you bought them, you may want to depreciate the purchase instead. I mentioned depreciation in the chapter on financial documents. Depreciating means you take the expense over time rather than in only the year of purchase. The length of time is based on an IRS table and set by the asset's useful life.

For a simple example, imagine you purchased an asset for $1,000 that has a 10-year depreciation schedule and no value at the end of the period of time. You could take $100 a year for 10 years rather than $1,000 in a single year. If you need to make an expensive purchase and you don't have much income, depreciation may be better than expensing. A word of caution—depreciation rules get complicated in a hurry. Talk to a tax professional to be sure you understand them.

You should be able to deduct the cost of anything directly related to expenses around your creative endeavor. For example, you could claim the cost of writing supplies, art materials, and dancing shoes.

Technology expenses can often be deducted but only up to the percent you are using the items for your creative endeavor. If you're a writer and purchase a laptop only for writing, you could deduct all of it. If you use it for other purposes, as well, you are likely only eligible for a partial deduction. The same goes for printers, phones, ZOOM lights, and any other technology you need.

Classes, seminars, conventions, and associated travel expenses should be deductible. However, be careful claiming wildly expensive trips. Although some tax planning publications and podcasts encourage claiming every dime you can, I believe you want to maintain a degree of reasonableness as you do your return. You don't want the IRS to decide your creative endeavor isn't a business. Their classification could be very difficult to change.

Unfortunately, clothing is not deductible unless you wear a recognized uniform. A uniform is not what you decide your fans want to see you wear. It's a specific outfit required by an employer. Dry cleaning isn't deductible when you are at home, but it is a deductible expense while you are traveling.

Meals and snacks are only fully deductible if food is available for public events, like an art show. Otherwise, business meals or meals eaten during travel are fifty percent deductible.

If you drive your vehicle to an event, you can take a deduction for each mile you drive. In 2024, the deduction was .67 cents per mile. Alternatively, you can list all the actual vehicle expenses and do your own calculation. You might receive a bigger deduction, but you must decide if the difference is worth the work. Use a mapping app to justify the length of the trip. That, along with your event marketing, should provide enough documentation if you are claiming mileage.

Other travel expenses must pass the IRS test of ordinary, necessary, and reasonable. The purpose of the trip must be business, not pleasure. This applies even if you conduct some business, like talking to a bookstore or art gallery, while traveling.

The IRS is particularly concerned with foreign trips deemed business expenses. Short trips may be easier to deduct, but for longer trips, you can only engage in personal events twenty-five percent of the time. If you spend more time than this on personal activities, you can only deduct the business-specific expenses.

These deductions are not an exhaustive list, and I have only provided summary explanations. You don't want to get sideways with the tax code, so if you have unusual deductions, you will want to talk to a tax professional who specializes in working with creatives. This person can give you more details.

Activity

I like a good tax deduction as much as the next person. Additionally, I believe you should run your creative pursuit as a business if possible. Still, look at taking reasonable deductions, and depreciate any expensive equipment if your income is lower. If you aren't sure how much you can take, talk to a CPA who specializes in working with creatives. Jot your ideas on the following lines.

26

HOME OFFICES

arta wrote from home. She had a separate space with her standing desk, a printer, and a mug warmer. She didn't do anything else while she was there, and she was excited to discover this would allow her to claim a home office deduction. She wasn't sure how to find the rules about what she could take.

As a creative, you likely have a home studio or office long before you rent professional space. In fact, depending on your medium, you may always use only a home office. Did you know that you can deduct the cost of your home office from your tax liability? The Internal Revenue Service gives you two ways of claiming it: the simplified option or the regular method.

Whichever way you choose, the hardest part of being able to take the home office deduction is the exclusivity of use requirement. Whatever space you choose for your office cannot be used for anything else. For example, you cannot use a guest bedroom as a home office even if you only have guests once a year. If you don't have a whole room, you can take part of a room as a home office if you only use that part for your creative endeavor.

If you can meet that qualification, the rules between the simplified and regular methods begin to differ. In the simplified version, you can only take 300 square feet, and you can only claim $5 per square foot. This limits your deduction to $1,500. However, in the regular method, you can take the actual percentage of your home used along with actual expenses that you verify through records.

In the regular method, you can take the percentage of any major cost or expense in your home that is applicable to your home office or studio. For example, if you purchase a new roof, and your home office is fifteen percent of the square footage of your home, then fifteen percent of the new roof is deductible. You can continue this with most home expenses like repairs, lawn service, and house cleaning.

It sounds too good to be true, doesn't it? Here's the catch. Your home office deduction can never exceed your income, whichever way you choose to calculate it. Whether you're using the simplified version with the $1,500 maximum deduction or the regular method that allows potentially more, if you only earn $1,000, that is all the home office deduction you can claim. And that assumes you had no other expenses. If you have zeroed out your income with other costs, you can't take a home office deduction at all.

Here's a tip. If you are getting your business off the ground and still struggling, take the home office deduction last. You want to be able to show the IRS that you are trying to make a profit. If you zero out your income by only taking the home office deduction, you can't show them things you are pursuing to try to become cash flow positive.

The regular method has some other limitations, as well. For every dollar you take in deduction, you must recapture that amount when you sell your house. In English, this means that the IRS gives you $250,000 of tax-free profit on your primary residence (home) if you're single and $500,000 if you're married. So, if you sell your home for $300,000, and you paid $100,000 when you bought it, you have no taxable gain on the sale of your home because $300,000-$100,000=$200,000. Two hundred thousand is less than the smallest phaseout for deduction.

Let's look at what would happen if you took the regular home office deduction. Assume over the course of your career, you took $70,000 in home office deductions because you had been successful and could deduct that much. The $70,000 would adjust the basis of your house down from $100,000 to $30,000. Now, if you sold it for $300,000, you would have $270,000 of gain, and assuming you're single, the last $20,000 of gain would be subject to capital gains tax.

For most people, this adjustment to your home's price, called an "adjustment to basis" in finance terms, isn't large enough to cause an issue. If so, you may decide paying the capital gains tax is worth it, especially if you have no intention of selling your house. Still, it's something to think about before you trigger potential taxes.

If you use the simplified method, your $1,500 deduction makes no difference to the price of your house. Of course, it's also not a large deduction if you're a successful creative, and you may find taking the standard home office deduction to your benefit. Again, either choice is fine, but you want to know why you are making your decisions.

For artists who are earlier in their careers but still getting value from the deduction, the simplified deduction is probably the best. As your profitability increases, you should invest in a good CPA who can help you decide how to proceed. If you're somewhere in the middle and don't have enough money to hire a CPA, more information than you ever wanted to know can be found in IRS Publication 587: www.irs.gov/publications/p587.

Activity

If you don't have a home office, do you have space to set one up? Would you benefit more from the simplified deduction or the traditional method? Jot your ideas on the following lines.

_____

_____

_____

_____

_____

_____

_____

_____

27

INCOME TAXES

va wasn't trying to break tax laws. Keeping up with what she owed the IRS was more complicated after she didn't have an employer to take care of it. Laying back money and paying her taxes quarterly was hard to do when other bills vied for her attention. She hoped she was paying enough, but she needed a better system.

I'm not sure who said, "There's nothing certain but death and taxes." Benjamin Franklin gets the credit, but the inevitability of both events goes back several thousand years. Ancient civilizations charged taxes that citizens had to pay, and we all know that no one dodges the Grim Reaper forever.

If income taxes are a certainty, how do we deal with them as an unavoidable part of earning money from our creative pursuits? Don't get overwhelmed. It's not that difficult.

If you are a traditional employee, your employer withholds taxes and payroll taxes from your paycheck. You receive the amount of your earnings left over after these taxes are paid. Your paycheck is called your "net pay," and you don't have to do much paperwork to receive it.

When you are a creative and earn money in a gig economy environment, doing your taxes is more work. We'll talk about payroll taxes in more detail in another chapter, so here, I'm going to talk about how to pay your income tax liability.

First, if you earn more than $400 overall from your creative work, you must pay income taxes. So if you earned $200, $300, and $100 over three different events, you would owe income tax on $600. Any expenses you incurred would offset the gross income, but you still must report what you made.

If you receive a 1099 form, likely in the form of a 1099 MISC (for miscellaneous), that income is reported differently on your taxes than the money you receive directly. It's still taxable, but you will list it on a different part of your return. The income I'm talking about here is usually going to be cash, checks, credit card purchases, or cash app transactions.

If you earn income that exceeds your expenses, you must pay quarterly taxes. For example, if you earn $500 during the first calendar quarter of the year and you also incur $100 of expenses, you would make a tax payment for that quarter on $400. You would repeat this process for each quarter in which you had income.

The IRS has multiple ways for you to make payments. If you have another job that pays you regularly, you can have additional taxes withheld from your paycheck sufficient to cover your gig income.

If you don't have another job, then you likely will complete IRS form 1040-ES for your quarterly estimated taxes. The IRS provides instructions for completing it.

If this gives you a headache, you could use a payroll service that would withhold the income tax and, as a bonus, also pay your employment tax for you. You deposit your gross earnings in an account that is tied to the service. Then, each month, you request a paycheck for the amount you earned. The payroll service handles the income and payroll taxes. Of course, payroll services aren't free. However, costs are dropping, and the gig economy has encouraged the services to broaden how they can help people.

You could also hire a bookkeeper or CPA to handle your taxes, as well, but this is also not free. Today's software provides a more affordable option for most people. Of course, if you are financially successful, you probably need a CPA anyway, and that person can calculate your estimated taxes or recommend someone affordable.

With just a little practice, you can handle your tax paper-work. The most important thing to remember is that the taxes are due. You don't want to owe the IRS money and not pay it. Taxes, interest, and penalties just aren't worth it.

Activity

Keep records of your income and expenses. You will likely need to pay quarterly taxes unless you have another job where you earn a paycheck. You can have your creative busi-ness taxes deducted from that paycheck and avoid quarterly filing. Jot some notes on the following lines.

_____

_____

_____

28

SALES TAX

*M*aya made jewelry. She tried to price it so people *could afford to make purchases. As a result, she had several sales every month. Some were credit card or cash app purchases, but some were just cash. She had registered with her state's sales tax office, but she had a terrible time remembering to log in and pay the tax each month. She also sold through her website, and she wondered how she should be handling the tax on out-of-state purchases.*

When you create items like books or art and you sell them yourself, you may need to collect sales tax. The rules around sales tax are complicated, and you need to consult your own tax professionals to determine your liability. Still, there are some large categories you need to understand: sales tax in your own state, out-of-state sales, and virtual sales. Remember that this information only applies if you are selling your items. You likely have no liability if anyone else is selling for you and collecting sales tax from the purchasers.

Your first step is to create a sales tax account in the state where you live. You will need to contact your state sales tax office and review the process. Often, you create your account online, and the process is simple. Each month, you go into that account and report your earnings. If you earned nothing, you still complete the online report. However, if you made sales, you specify the part of the state where the sale occurred, and the portal should automatically calculate your liability. Often, you can attach a credit card or a bank account and pay the taxes immediately.

If you have traveled to an out-of-state event, the rules become more complicated. I strongly encourage you to seek assistance beyond the scope of this book. My goal is to show you where you might have a problem. Your goal is to solve it accurately!

Again, remember that if sales are being made through a central vendor and tax is being collected, you are probably in compliance. The vendor pays you the difference between the price of your item, their cut, and any tax they have paid. As long as the state receives the tax, you don't have to worry about it.

However, let's assume you don't want to pay the vendor, and the event allows you to make your own, direct sales. Now, you must look at the event state's nexus rules. "Nexus" is a Latin word that translates as "to bind" or "to tie." If you have nexus in the other state, you must pay sales tax to it. Unfortunately, selling items at a festival, conference, or convention often creates nexus, regardless of the value of the sale. As a result, you probably are required to pay sales tax to that state. Remember that sales tax is always paid to the state where the sale is made, not the state where you live. See if the state offers a one-time tax return for minimal sales. Otherwise, you may have to file periodic reports with the state, even if the numbers are nothing but zero.

I know this rule is often ignored by creatives and many other people, too. However, my goal is to provide you with accurate information. If you have an out-of-state event, contact the event coordinator and ask how they are going to handle sales tax. You may decide that running through the vendor is the best solution if possible.

The final scenario I want to mention is selling your items through your website, giving you the status of a remote seller with potential economic nexus. That sounds like a mouthful, but the rule is quite beneficial for smaller merchants. Most states create a minimum number of sales or a gross sales number before you owe sales tax. The gross sales often begin at $100,000, with some states higher than that. The number of transactions sometimes includes the gross sales and sometimes is in place of it. The most restrictive minimums as of the writing of this book are 200 sales or $100,000. For small creatives, these numbers likely exceed their virtual sales in that state. Remember that these rules apply to online sales only.

No doubt sales tax is confusing! If you sell a physical product, you need to take some time to review the requirements in more detail. I'm also providing you with an online resource I found helpful. https://www.avalara.com/us/en/learn.html Be aware that Avalara offers a sales tax service. However, I am not currently a subscriber, and I'm not suggesting you should enroll either. However, sales tax is complicated, and their information is up-to-date and easy to understand. Don't ignore sales tax requirements. If you stay organized as you go, you won't get overwhelmed.

Activity

If you only make sales in your home state, paying sales tax may be nagging, but it isn't difficult. However, the minute you make out-of-state sales, the process gets complicated. Take time to ask the event coordinator about sales tax treatment before each of the events. Talk to a CPA or bookkeeper who works with creatives to be sure you are handling everything correctly. Jot your ideas on the following lines.

_____

_____

_____

_____

_____

_____

_____

_____

_____

29

KEEPING RECORDS

*R*obert couldn't figure out how he was the son of a CPA *and a bank vice president. His parents were so orga-nized. When he was very young, he would see his mom balance her checkbook at the kitchen table. Now, she did it online, but she still kept boxes of organized paper receipts. Every year, as Robert was completing the taxes for his mural painting business, he scrambled to find his income and expenses. He felt like he cheated himself every year. Once the taxes were done, he tried to organize his data, but he hoped he never got audited. He wasn't sure he'd be able to find what he needed.*

Accurate information is key to running your creative endeavor like a business. Not keeping records creates a crisis when you are filing your taxes, making an insurance claim, or applying for a loan.

When you file your taxes, you must be able to prove your amount of income and expenses to the IRS. Proving income requires making copies of checks, organizing online payment methods, and accurately reporting the cash you receive. If you take credit cards or use a cash app, both services provide documents showing your income history.

131

Try to save them monthly, as data over a year old can be harder to organize. Many of them only provide links for the previous twelve months, although the earlier numbers can be obtained if necessary. Physical cash is trickier, but if you give your customer a receipt, that also provides proof for the Internal Revenue Service (IRS).

Tracking your expenses can be difficult, because you are more likely to acquire paper receipts that you don't want to lose. If you purchase something with cash, that receipt is your only record. If you're like me, it's easy to drop those receipts into a bag, purse, or vehicle. Suddenly, they're gone!

I take pictures of receipts I don't want to lose, and then I send the picture to myself as an email with a subject line explaining the expense. It sounds cumbersome, but the whole process takes about thirty seconds on my phone, and I don't have to worry about losing anything. Of course, what you pay for with a credit card or cash app automatically provides you with records. Download them monthly.

In addition to calculating your taxes, you also need to keep records if your purchase requires insurance. You must be able to prove how much something costs if you want someone else to replace the correct value. Of course, if you have purchased an appreciating asset (like a non-electronic musical instrument), you may need to get the item periodically appraised to account for the increase in value.

You also need to be able to prove the price of something if you want to borrow money to pay for it. Of course, any initial financier will know the price, but if you want better loan terms or if interest rates drop, you may need to refinance. You will need documentation of the cost or pay for a new appraisal.

Keeping records doesn't end when you file your taxes, acquire insurance, or apply for a loan. Obviously, you will need records to file an insurance claim or refinance. Perhaps most importantly, if you are audited by the IRS, you will want up-to-date loan payment information.

The rules around how long to keep tax return documentation are complicated. I'm going to simplify them for you by giving you some worst-case scenarios. First, if you have knowingly committed tax fraud, you need to keep your documentation forever. True tax fraud is quite rare. Usually, people tend to forget to include income in their tax returns, or they misunderstand the tax code.

Certain types of tax errors can trigger audits up to six years after filing your tax return, even though three years is the common statute of limitations for a traditional audit. Because the six-year audit involves under-reported income, I recommend that you keep your documentation for six years for any income that you received without an accompanying tax document, like a W2 or 1099.

According to the IRS, you should keep your filed tax returns forever. Of course, you don't need to keep them in paper form. You can keep them as electronic documents, or if you receive your tax return from a CPA, ask them for an electronic copy. Although CPA firms are conscientious, don't assume they are keeping your records. Firms can be purchased, partners can die, and people can retire. Trust the firm to file the return, but keep the documents, yourself.

Keeping records can be burdensome; however, having proof of what you earned and what you paid is critical to the success of your creative business. Take time to stay organized regularly, and you will have less of a mess come tax time.

Activity

I don't care how you do it, but you need to organize your finances. Keep paper files or take pictures with your phone and store everything online. Just find a way to create a permanent archive of your income and expenses. Jot your ideas on the following lines.

ESTATE

30

POWERS OF ATTORNEY

*R*onaldo knew his wife would be devastated if he should become seriously ill. Still, she was the only one he trusted to make decisions about his healthcare. However, his foundry created a different situation. His wife would want to be helpful, but he wasn't sure she knew enough about his business to make decisions. His assistant knew the bills as well as he did, and Ronaldo felt confident she could keep things going until he was able to return to work.

It's easy to think we'll live forever. However, we know that isn't true. Sometimes, it's harder to imagine that we might become permanently, or even temporarily, incapacitated. Physical incapacity is a tragedy, but mental incapacity can send your financial life into freefall. If you couldn't think clearly, who would see that your bills were paid? Who would ensure you received the medical care you wanted?

Fortunately, legal documents exist to handle both situations. Powers of attorney for finance and healthcare allow you to choose who makes decisions on your behalf.

A power of attorney can be permanent or springing. If it's permanent, the named individual always holds the ability to make financial or healthcare decisions. This choice is most common in committed relationships like marriages or partnerships.

On the other hand, springing powers of attorney go into effect when the holder becomes incapacitated. Medical professionals determine the incapacity, and often the decision requires the consensus of two or more physicians.

Springing powers of attorney are valuable for people who want to remain in control of their decisions until a time of crisis. They are more common when the holder has concerns about turning over full power to another individual. Some people are concerned with any document that gives another person authority. However, remember that incapacitated individuals cannot conduct financial transactions, make medical decisions, or handle day-in, day-out situations. If something happens to you and you don't have a power of attorney in place, your finances could collapse, and your healthcare preferences could be ignored.

As I mentioned earlier, spouses or partners often hold stronger powers of attorney. They are also more likely to share banking accounts. Additionally, the healthcare system tends to value the opinion of a spouse; however, partners have no such deference. Blood-related family members will have their opinions followed before non-spouse partners, regardless of the length of the relationship. This presents unique challenges for unmarried couples. If the relatives and the partner agree on treatment, there is usually no crisis. However, sometimes a partner has better insight, or sometimes relatives can have a contentious relationship with the partner. Then, an already tragic situation gets even worse.

Lack of access to funds can also become a crisis, because most people live a lifestyle that requires both incomes. If one person becomes incapacitated for an extended period, the other partner could lose the home and possessions, like cars, because money may not be accessible to pay the bills. This is most problematic for couples who maintain separate bank accounts.

One final consideration is that the same person doesn't have to hold all the powers of attorney. I saw a situation where the creator named his spouse as the medical power of attorney but gave a friend the power of attorney to run the business. He told me he believed his spouse would not be able to run the business, but he wanted her to take care of his medical needs. He had spoken with her, and she agreed with his concerns.

Most people need some kind of financial and medical power of attorney. Talk to the person or people you are considering for those roles. Make sure they are comfortable with the level of responsibility. Additionally, talk to your estate attorney for recommendations or further considerations. You want the documents to be in place before you have a crisis.

Activity

Take some time to decide who you would want to make healthcare decisions for you if you were unable to speak for yourself. Who would you want to make financial decisions? Remember, when you create powers of attorney for healthcare and finance, you don't need to give one person all the responsibility. Your spouse, partner, or friend might make your medical decisions and your personal financial decisions, while a creative peer assists with your business finances. Remember talk to these people before you list them on your documents, and explain why you made your decisions, so there aren't any surprises. Jot your notes on the following lines.

31

ADVANCED DIRECTIVES

Estelle was old enough to remember the Terri Schiavo case. Sometimes, as she worked on her novel in the early morning light, she shook her head. She still couldn't believe that the US Congress and President thought they had the right to decide the future of that young girl who entered a persistent, vegetative state. Terri lay unresponsive in her bed day after day as her boyfriend, parents, her parents' minister, Congress, and the President of the United States fought over her treatment. Estelle knew young people never thought they would die, but they would. She, herself, had created an advanced directive so her kids wouldn't have to make those decisions. She would go out on her own terms.

Powers of attorney let people you trust make medical and financial decisions on your behalf, often when you are incapacitated. Having these documents in place gives you peace of mind that your life will not fall apart if you can't take care of things.

However, end-of-life decisions can be very stressful for someone serving as your medical power of attorney (POA). By creating an advanced directive, sometimes called a "living will," you can remove the burden from your POA by making your own decisions should you become gravely ill.

An advanced directive is a legal document where you indicate what extraordinary measures will be taken if you are in a persistent vegetative state or have suffered a dire medical emergency. Do you want a ventilator? Do you want nutrition through a feeding tube and/or hydration through an IV? Do you want your heart restarted if it stops?

State documents vary broadly in how they structure advanced directives. You will want to look them up yourself or consult an attorney. If you already have an advanced directive, make sure it's still up to date. In Oklahoma, living wills are available from the state online. However, a change in the state document language rendered many existing directives null and void. Again, this can be a question for your attorney.

Remember that an advanced directive isn't a moral document that doesn't need to be "all or nothing." You can review the options and accept some of them while rejecting others. For example, you might want hydration but not nutrition. If you believe life is sacred and should be preserved, this document allows you to express your wish for food, water, a ventilator, and resuscitation. The document can be crafted to your needs.

Although I think advanced directives are valuable, there is one final recommendation I would make. Remember that when you put an advanced directive into place, it overrides the wishes of your chosen power of attorney and other family members. Although your end-of-life decisions are always your choice, gather the people you love and explain your choices to them. The importance of this became evident during COVID. Ventilators were common tools the medical community used to try to save lives. Review the language around the use of life-extending measures and share your desires with those you love. If your tribe wants to be the ones to make the medical decision, that's a conversation you need to have.

Advanced directives allow you to control the end of your life without putting the burden on those you love. Read the documents, be sure anything you've created is up-to-date, and ensure that everyone knows your wishes. When you need the document, your emotions will be strong.

Activity

As part of your estate plan, you should consider including an advanced directive. If you already have one, be sure your state hasn't changed the language requirements. Then, share your wishes with the people you love, so you can have any necessary conversations. Jot your notes on the following lines.

_____

_____

_____

_____

_____

32

WILLS AND TRUSTS

efore he began to pursue his sculpting full time, Bill had been a business major and worked in the office of a regional corporation. He wasn't afraid of numbers, and he enjoyed creating business solutions to enhance his sales. However, making an estate plan terrified him. He knew he was being irrational, but he feared creating his will. So, he continued to postpone calling an attorney.

After you die, who do you want to inherit your possessions? Your spouse, your partner, your kids, or your friends? You should take steps now to ensure that your legacy is passed down in ways that lower the transfer expenses.

A will is a basic legal document that describes how your possessions will be distributed after your death. In a will, you provide the list of your assets and the beneficiaries of each item. Wills are important documents, because, without them, your wishes might not be followed.

If you die without a will, you die intestate. Dying intestate means that the state decides who receives your possessions. The decision isn't haphazard. Each state has a very similar beneficiary table that spells out the order of inheritance.

According to the state, if you are not married, your partner isn't automatically entitled to anything. If you are legally married, your partner is your default beneficiary if you don't have a will. This legal status is one of the reasons why the ability to marry is so important.

Of course, if you aren't married, you can list your partner as your beneficiary, and he or she will receive your property. Additionally, with a will, you can give different possessions to different beneficiaries, so you can provide for parents, children, partners, and friends.

Unfortunately, having a will doesn't protect your assets from probate. Probate is the legal process to ensure your financial obligations are met. If you die with probatable assets, before they can be distributed according to your wishes, they must go through probate to determine that your beneficiaries can receive them. Probate is announced in publications like newspapers, so debtors can come and make claims before the assets are divided. Although probate is usually uneventful, it's public, costs money, and usually requires an attorney.

You can avoid probate in three different ways. Assets can be transferred outside of probate through titling, beneficiary, or trust. When an asset is transferred through titling, this means the owner of the asset has set up a beneficiary who automatically receives the asset after the owner dies. One type of titling that accomplishes this is Joint Tenancy with Right of Survivorship (JTWROS). The survivorship part of this titling keeps the asset out of probate. If you live in a community property state, you will have to be careful to title things in a way that allows survivorship.

The second way to avoid probate is through declaring a beneficiary. You may be familiar with beneficiaries through life insurance policies, Individual Retirement Accounts (IRAs), or other retirement plans. When you open these, the application asks you who should inherit the asset. When you die, your policy or account automatically goes to them. Additionally, some other kinds of financial assets can have a beneficiary by creating them as Transfer on Death (TOD) or Payable on Death (POD).

The third way to avoid probate is to place the asset in a trust. Trusts are complicated and should be opened with the advice of an attorney. Many trusts are created purely to avoid probate. Others allow the trust creator to slow the spending of assets, divide the same asset among multiple beneficiaries, or make charitable contributions. Different kinds of trusts meet different kinds of goals. You will want to talk to an attorney about all three strategies for avoiding probate or meeting other needs.

If none of these situations concern you, let me offer a final, critical reason to create a will or a trust. If you have children and you die without a document saying who will raise them, your state will decide. You may want your child raised by a partner or sibling, but your state may require that your child be raised by your parent. No one wants their children raised by anyone other than the person of their choice. For that reason alone, take some time to create the document with an attorney.

I have clients who are excellent with their finances, but they avoid creating an estate plan. I think subconsciously, they believe that the document will lead to their death. It won't. Create an estate plan today, so the people you love won't struggle in the future.

Activity

You need an estate plan. You need to be sure that the people you love inherit your possessions. Sometimes, our desires are different than those of the state, especially if we have a partner and not a spouse. Take some time to make a plan and jot your notes on the following lines.

_____

_____

_____

_____

_____

_____

_____

_____

_____

33

INTELLECTUAL PROPERTY

aria knew that most of her assets would go to her chosen beneficiaries after she died. She had resolved her estate issues by titling some of her assets jointly, and she had beneficiaries on her retirement accounts. She had even added a transfer on death to her bank account. However, she had no way to handle the copyrights of her compositions. They were hers, and if she died, they would go to whomever was her closest heir. She made an appointment to talk with an estate attorney. She didn't know if she needed a will or a trust, but she knew she needed something.

We talked about the basics of wills and trusts in the last chapter, but here, I want to talk specifically about protecting your intellectual property after your death. Intellectual property includes copyrights, patents, trademarks, trade secrets, and industrial designs. You probably don't have a trade secret, but you may own several copyrights and trademarks. Ignoring the intellectual property in your estate will lead to issues for your heirs.

Intellectual property lives longer than you do. Right now, copyrights survive seventy years after the date of death of the creator. You want the people you love to benefit financially from your hard work, so you want to be sure they receive the assets after you die. Once they have ownership, they can hold the rights or sell them.

Intellectual property is intangible, and cannot have a beneficiary or a joint ownership potential. Inheriting intellectual property is usually handled through a will or a trust. If it is held in a will, the property will be subject to probate. We talked briefly about the probate process in the last chapter. Remember that probate requires a judge to determine that debts are paid and that assets go to the person intended. Probate is stressful, time-consuming, and relatively expensive.

If you own intellectual property, you will want to talk with an estate attorney who works with creatives. You may want to place the property inside of a trust to ensure the beneficiary and avoid the probate process. I'm not an attorney, so I'm not going to recommend anything specific. However, an estate attorney can help you with any details.

Activity

Dying with items outside a beneficiary creates issues for your heirs. If you have copyrights or other intellectual property, you should contact a local estate attorney to determine how to handle it. While you're there, give your entire estate plan a quick checkup. After you die, you won't be able to fix it if you have made a mistake. Jot your notes on the following lines.

OTHER

34

ADVOCACY

*E*leanor had marched in the sixties and seventies for equal rights and social justice. Now, she was decades older, but she still stayed involved in political issues that were important to her. She encouraged her younger friends to study the issues and vote, too. She believed every voice was important.

In a nation where arts education feels like it's under fire... In your world that is often portrayed as flighty and not business oriented... As a financial consumer who must negotiate with advisers who don't want to be your fiduciary... you must be an advocate for your rights. I believe you should also join organizations that have similar missions to your own.

Although hanging out with your tribe is important, you should take your arts advocacy further. Each discipline has professional organizations that hold arts advocacy as their only goal or as a main pillar of their beliefs.

You may be aware of some of these, while other creatives with more experience in your discipline can guide you toward worthy organizations. Again, you want to be cautious. There are frauds and scams in this world, too.

However, with just a little research, you should be able to find the legitimate ones.

These organizations may advocate on behalf of an entire creative genre, or they may be more focused. For example, in the world of writing, there are advocacy groups for all writers. There is also an organization that focuses on women who write crime, because, historically, they have had difficulty breaking into this genre. Your creative world may work much the same way. Look for the big organizations along with the more specific ones.

You may also find groups that are adjacent to what you do in your discipline. Or you may want to support organizations that support all of the arts. Feel free to branch out to these, as well. These groups, ranging from exactly what you do to national, multi-genre endeavors, are advocating to keep our world reading, painting, sculpting, singing, dancing, acting, and all those other glorious disciplines that make life worth living.

You also need to vote. I wouldn't begin to tell you how to vote, but you need to pay attention to what is happening in the political world. Who supports the arts? Who doesn't? Who will make your life better? Worse? And finally, who will look out for your financial best interest?

We talked about considerations when choosing financial professionals. Those individuals, both good and self-serving, influence politicians, as well. They also have their own organizations. Remember how we talked about the fiduciary standard? Unfortunately, the lobbies against the fiduciary standard are larger than the groups in favor of it. The fiduciary world is bogged down again in late 2024, when I'm writing this book. I'm hopeful the standard will become mandatory, but I'm not confident.

What I know is that we can all look for lawmakers and candidates who believe that the people who work with your money should hold a fiduciary standard with it. You should have confidence that every time you give your money to someone, they will do the best they can without any consideration of their own compensation. Additionally, they will disclose all the money they received for recommending a product.

I can't believe I have to write those words. Earlier, I told you when I entered finance, I just assumed that was the way the system worked. I was wrong, and that belief is still wrong.

Of course, voting is complex, and you will have many issues you care about. However, I hope the behavior of your financial professional crosses your mind as you cast your ballot. You deserve to be able to trust anyone who helps you with your investments.

Activity

Look for accurate sources of information and stay informed about the issues that impact your life. Keep up with legislation that impacts your money, too.

35
FINDING YOUR TRIBE

When Geoff began to dance in grade school, his classes had boys and girls. As he continued dancing, he began to feel more isolated in his high school. The creative people hung together, and Geoff was relieved to graduate. Once he got to college, he found many young dancers just like him. They studied together, rehearsed at the same time, and even shared audition information. They became a second family.

Few people like to live in a vacuum. Sometimes, we might feel like the people around us don't understand us. They don't understand our drive or passion for our creative endeavor. They may not even understand our willingness to take less money to pursue our craft.

When we are isolated, we can get depressed, feel like we aren't good enough, and wonder if we should continue in our career path. "Imposter syndrome," the feeling that you are not as good as your peers, is common in all professions. In fact, the unfair thing about imposter syndrome, in my non-trained opinion, is that the people most susceptible seem to be those who are trying the hardest. In other words, the people who should feel the least like imposters often suffer the most.

One of the best ways to counteract the isolation and feelings of inadequacy is to get around people like you—your tribe. Your tribe will understand your feelings of inadequacy or the sense that not everyone understands you. Tribes can be virtual, local, or national, and you can begin to establish these bonds in several different ways.

Almost no good came out of COVID-19, but the ability to create virtual relationships is an exception. For people with limited mobility and resources, ZOOM has been a blessing. Social media groups on different sites have members are interested in almost anything. If you're homebound, look for a ZOOM event.

Additionally, look for free or inexpensive local gatherings of people like you. Maybe your city does a monthly art show. Maybe you could attend a concert at the local university and talk to people during intermission. Maybe there's a local writing group you could join. You won't make best friends instantly, but you will begin to be part of a community that thinks like you do.

You can also go to local galleries, music stores, and bookstores. And don't forget your local library. Libraries today are just cool, offering talks, technology lessons, and often labs with sound rooms and 3-D printers. Although they are still pretty quiet, nearly every stereotype you have about a library is gone. Hang out and talk to people. Ask about upcoming events.

If you're older, see what activities are offered at a community senior center. We have a new one in my town, and I'm amazed at all the different creative activities they offer. Growing older no longer means sitting on the porch or playing dominos.

Once you have committed to making your creative

endeavor a major part of your life, look at larger, national organizations. These people are struggling with the same things you are, and they likely have beginners' sections. They also may offer free resources that you can access if you can't afford the dues.

Finally, begin looking for local events where you can have a presence. If you have reached out the way I've suggested, you know some people who are actively creating. Find out where they show, sell, or perform. See if you can have a presence, too. Attending these events as a creative will put you in front of the public, and you will begin to grow stronger bonds with the other participants.

As a new author, I participated in an event with writers who had many books published. I listened more than I talked. I learned that even people I consider wildly successful have the same concerns I have. Even when we work in different genres, we love the same things about our craft. I found my tribe, and it benefitted my writing and my personal life in many ways. If you aren't plugged into your tribe yet, take some time to find it. I promise it's out there. They're waiting for you to arrive!

Activity

As a creative, you will want to get involved in local groups and organizations. You may also find an online community. Listen, be enthusiastic, and become an active member. As you make friends, you will find a group of people who are allies and supporters. Jot your ideas on the following lines.

_____

_____

_____

_____

_____

_____

_____

36

PHYSICAL AND MENTAL
PROSPERITY

*E*very time her best friend made a sale, Yvonne felt her stress level rising. They had gone to art school together, made equivalent grades, and had stalls in the same studio. Yvonne wasn't jealous, but she believed her friend seemed more successful than she was. Even when she tried to convince herself she was wrong, that didn't stop the tension from rising up her neck. It also didn't make getting out of bed any easier. Her stress was almost debilitating.

When I went into finance, I needed a phrase that people would find easy to remember. I chose "Plan Your Prosperity!" I love the word "prosperity." We all know that everyone can't be rich. In fact, certain life choices almost ensure that although we might be comfortable, we won't live an extravagant life. But we can be prosperous, because prosperity is much more than money.

Of course, to be prosperous, you need a level of financial security, but prosperity is broader than that. Prosperity is being surrounded by people you love, whether that's family or friends. Prosperity is doing work you find meaningful. Prosperity even includes your fur, feather, or scale family.

Prosperity also involves two other important factors: your mental and physical health. Your mind and body are important, and you need to take steps to ensure you are living your best life.

An important goal is to control your stress level. Meditate, pray, or find another way to center yourself. Additionally, talk to professionals if you are struggling with depression or other mental or emotional issues. Personal or virtual appointments are possible today, and thanks to the Affordable Care Act, mental and behavioral health services are deemed essential health benefits that must be covered by insurance. If you don't know how to choose someone, talk to your doctor or a friend for recommendations.

Physical health is also important, and it's so easy to ignore. Eat healthy food regularly and get some physical activity each day. You don't need to walk or jog miles. Just find something you enjoy doing. If you're not in shape, check with your physician and start with short periods of time. Between fit watches and health apps, you can track your steps, diet, and even your water consumption. The external reinforcement provided by the app may help you stay on target. You can also create a goal with a friend and remain accountable to each other.

Take time to get together with other people. It's easy to bury yourself in your studio and lose track of time; however, human interaction is important. Although introverts enjoyed the isolation of COVID-19, others suffered from loneliness. Take time to look for your tribe.

When your life is in balance, everything is better. In fact, you may find yourself staying up to date with your finances or making better decisions as other areas of your life come together. When we fall apart, we tend to fall apart everywhere. But by taking some steps to improve your mental and physical health, your creative endeavors may be more successful, too.

Activity

Taking care of your physical and mental health is important. Don't just ignore symptoms or believe they are part of being a creative. Today, online services make it easier to seek out affordable assistance. This world is a better place because you are in it. Take steps to prosper, not just survive. Jot some notes on the following lines.

37

TEACHING YOUR KIDS ABOUT MONEY

ori wanted her young daughter to understand money better than she had. Her mother and father never mentioned finances in front of her. She had overheard them talking about paying bills a few times, but she had no idea about the details. Her lack of money skills caused her difficulties when she moved out on her own. She didn't want to do the same thing to her little girl.

In an earlier chapter, we talked about creating inexpensive memories with your kids. I believe in this concept so much. When I think back on my childhood, the things we did are more memorable than the gifts I received.

Still, it can be difficult to tell your children no when they ask for something. It's worse if you've been working long hours and feel bad about not spending enough time with them. Or maybe you're divorced, and your ex lavishes presents because he or she earns more money.

Kids don't always understand why mom or dad doesn't have the ability to purchase everything. If your child wants an expensive toy, you may have to explain that you can't buy it right now. It's hard, but honest conversations about money will help them grow up to be financially responsible adults.

Remember to keep your conversations about money age-appropriate. You can help young children understand how much items cost by comparing the amount to their allowance if they get one. They may be too young to relate the cost of items to your earnings. However, if you are comfortable sharing your personal finances with your older children, you can show them how long you must work to be able to buy something they want. Children don't mean to be thoughtless; they just have no actual comprehension of cost. Sadly, neither do some adults!

If you don't feel comfortable sharing your financial information with your kids, that's fine. But in a world where we will talk about literally anything but money, the conversations should probably happen at some point. However, it's up to you about when and how much you share.

Outside of explaining your finances, you can help your kids, even teenagers, learn the value of a dollar by having "saving money" contests. If you make sandwiches rather than eating out, help them calculate how much money you saved. Then, put ten percent back towards a special meal or activity. Once the cost of the expense is saved, they get the reward.

You may be surprised at how often the reward changes as you are saving money. This brings up an issue that is true for everyone but especially children. We see things every day that we think we want. Usually, if we wait a while, we realize the item was an impulse desire, and we move on. Our children can also be susceptible. They see something online or on television, and they want it. Too often, especially if parents are feeling stressed or pressured, they buy the item almost immediately. If it's close to the holidays, they may lay it back as a gift, only to have their child want something else the next day.

To avoid frustration, wait a few days before you make any purchases. See if the proposed present becomes the subject of a recurring theme or a one-time idea. I'm not going to tell you how much you can spend on gifts, but I do believe you should only buy your children what they need or what they really want. One or two gifts that they love will make them happier than a dozen "meh" items.

Additionally, I think it's a good idea to teach your children to give along with receiving. Take them to the dollar store and let them pick out one item apiece for the immediate people they love. Give them the money in advance (or let it come from their allowance), and calculate the costs of everything as you go. By shopping in a dollar store, the items can't get too expensive. You aren't doing this to get them to give a gift to you or your partner. You're teaching them how to be a giver.

There are so many financial topics, and often, they are not taught regularly in schools. If you want your children to learn more, check out the resources on the Council for Economic Education family program page: https://www.councilforeconed.org/programs/for-families/.

You can also find resources on the Kansas City Federal Reserve page: https://www.kansascityfed.org/ten/financial-literacy-tools-and-materials/.

Activity

Even very young children can begin to learn about money by playing games and coloring coins on https://kids.usmint.gov/. You can help older kids learn to save their allowance to buy price-appropriate items they want. Finally, if you feel comfortable sharing more about your financial condition with your teens, you can help them better understand the cost of living. Use the resources in this chapter to make the process easier.

_____

_____

_____

_____

_____

_____

_____

_____

_____

PART II

MONEY AND YOUR CREATIVE BUSINESS

3 8

BUSINESS STRUCTURES

an had been a photographer for years, and through hard work and a little luck, she had become quite successful. She always ran her business as a sole proprietorship, but she wondered if that was still a good idea. Jan was considering a more controversial show. Surely, no one would sue her! She also had an assistant who she wanted to help with retirement savings. She wanted to create a more robust business structure but didn't want to do anything too complicated.

If you want your creative work to be a business, you need to determine what business structure will be the most appropriate. You have several potentially good options, so let's look at each of them.

SOLE PROPRIETOR

The easiest business structure to open is the sole proprietorship. Opening a sole proprietorship requires nothing from you. You simply begin the activity. The lack of paperwork establishes that your venture isn't a separate legal entity. Instead, a sole proprietor owns the business and has the personal liability for the business debt. You can give your business a name other than your own, but that action has no legal implications and offers no personal liability protections.

The biggest advantage to a sole proprietorship is its ease of creation. You have no paperwork to submit to the state and no business tax return to file. Instead, you report your profits and expenses on Schedule C of your personal tax return.

However, there are two major risks to a sole proprietorship. First, you are personally liable for the business debt. If you become over-leveraged or run into any other financial trouble, you must pay back the debt. Your personal assets may be at risk. Formal business structures limit the debt liability to the assets of the business.

Further, if your business is sued, you are personally responsible for paying the lawsuit judgment amount if you lose the case. If, instead, your business was a legal entity, the business would be the recipient of the suit—not you, personally. You will need to weigh this concern carefully, as anyone can be sued. Even with these potential pitfalls, many small businesses are still sole proprietorships. Additionally, you might begin your venture as a sole proprietorship and change later as it grows.

PARTNERSHIPS

General partnerships are similar to sole proprietorships, except the business has more than one owner. They are easy to establish, since this business structure also does not have a legal identity. Partnerships have the same risks as sole proprietorships. Additionally, each partner is responsible for the actions of the other partners. Because this is a personal risk, be careful before you create a partnership.

A friend of mine used to tell me to "pick my partner before I picked my project." He urged caution when I was considering a business venture with another person. I think, over time, I have grown as wary as he was.

If you want to create a partnership, even if the person is a good friend, there are a few things to keep in mind. First, a written agreement should detail the responsibilities of everyone in the partnership. This includes formulas for sharing revenue and expenses, business functions like keeping the books and paying the bills, and administrative work.

The agreement should include what you will do if someone fails to keep their end of the bargain. And then, finally, before you sign anything, run the document by a lawyer to be sure nothing has been forgotten.

Being in a partnership has the advantage of not working alone and, potentially, having lower expenses. However, the wrong partner can create a nightmare. You lose control of your business while keeping the liability.

SUBCHAPTER S CORPORATIONS

If you want to create a true business structure, you might consider a Subchapter S Corporation (also called an S Corporation). Unlike sole proprietorships and partnerships, corporations are always legal entities. As a result, the owner is protected from personal liability for company debts. Additionally, the owner has greater personal protection in case of a lawsuit against the business.

Finally, if a business owner is attempting to raise money, shares of company stock can be sold to people willing to buy them. However, these stock sales don't happen frequently. Few people will want to risk purchasing part of your company, especially if you need money.

Remember, too, that once you have sold a share of corporate stock, you can't get it back. You don't want to sell so much stock that you no longer control your own business. The results can be downright catastrophic. The shareholders can take actions the founder doesn't like, including removing the founder from the company. Remember that owning a share of stock is the same as owning a piece of the business. Talk to an attorney before you decide to sell any shares.

An S corporation is just a corporation that has made a specific tax decision. The company makes a Subchapter S tax election, which requires the profits and losses from the business to flow through to the business owner or owners rather than being retained within the corporation. The S corporation must file a tax return, but corporate income tax is never due because of the corporation's flow-through nature.

What does the term "flow-through tax treatment" mean, exactly? The business earns income and incurs expenses. Once all the bills are paid, did the business make money? This profit or loss and a few other things are reported on a K-1 form. The data from the K-1 is then reported on the owner's personal tax return. If there are multiple owners, the gain/loss is divided by ownership percentage and reported on multiple K-1s.

S corporations are more complicated to create than sole props or partnerships. Paperwork must be filed with the state, annual corporate meetings must be held, and periodic state filings are required.

LIMITED LIABILITY COMPANIES

Limited Liability Companies (LLCs) are designed, as you might suspect, to help limit the business owner's liability. LLCs have enormous flexibility and fewer business structure requirements than S corporations. They are not, however, good vehicles for trying to raise capital, as shares cannot be sold.

Taxation is an important concern when considering an LLC. Members of an LLC that do not specifically choose to be taxed as a corporation are considered self-employed, not employees of the company. As a result, they will have to pay all their self-employment tax liability of Medicare and Social Security rather than share those expenses with the entity. If the LLC chooses to be taxed as a corporation, then the business pays half of the employment taxes, and the individual pays the other half. Choosing to be taxed as a corporation also allows the owners to defer more to their retirement accounts because they are not considered self-employed.

As you decide which business entity to select, start with two questions. The first is, "Do I need protection from lawsuits?" If so, you don't want to select a sole proprietorship or a partnership, as both of these entities cause you to retain all the risk.

The next question is, "How am I going to raise the funds to get my business off the ground?" If you are planning to sell shares, which is an unlikely occurrence, then you probably want to select a corporation with a subchapter S election.

Additionally, if you want to fund your retirement, a corporate structure helps you avoid net income from self-employment.

Once you have established your business structure, it's possible to change, but it's complicated. Take time now to get it right. You should talk to your attorney, CPA, and financial planner for the details of each option. Look at the advantages and disadvantages of each and choose the one most likely to help you meet your goals, both today and in the future.

Activity

If you are currently a sole proprietor, do you want a more formal business structure? Your two easiest options are forming a corporation and taking a sub-chapter S election or creating an LLC. LLCs can be taxed as a sole proprietorship or a corporation. Talk to your CPA and financial planner, and jot your ideas on the following lines.

_____

_____

_____

_____

_____

_____

_____

APPLYING FOR A BUSINESS NAME

red was excited to be transitioning his painting from a hobby to a business. He decided to call his company Fred's Fine Art, and he personalized shirts, hats, and pens with the name and a multi-colored paintbrush. He even bought an expensive sign for his gallery. He decided he should register his company as an LLC, but when he went to register the name with his state, he discovered another company was already using it. Fred not only had to rename his business, but he lost all his marketing efforts and swag, as well.

What do you want to call your creative endeavor? Is it just your name or something more complicated or meaningful to you? Anytime you are creating the name for a business, you should check first to see if the name is available. Then, before you file for it, think about it. Ask your friends and fellow creatives for their ideas. Remember that once you start to brand in a certain way, you are heading down a marketing path. Are you sure your name reflects not only who you are today but also where you think you are going?

It's a harder question than you might think. When I started writing, I branded everything as "Ask Peggy™." I still use this branding, including obtaining a trademark, for everything I do that involves personal finance. However, last year, I branched into also writing cozy mysteries. Unless you're asking me whodunnit, the branding isn't great. I'm updating my branding now, and I truly don't expect to go broader than these categories. Of course, I never thought I'd be writing mysteries, so who knows?

If you want to brand, the safest way is your name. You can probably use your name as the name of the business without any issues, although I would take several steps first. I would be sure that the name is available as a URL for your website, blog, social media, and anything else where you want to be found. If everything checks out, then you need to file the name of your business officially. As much as you can, name everything exactly alike. I have started a couple of social media sites under AskPeggy. I'm not changing them, but I wish I hadn't done that.

Fortunately, filing your business name is easy. All you do is register with your state and local government. You can likely find the application on your state's Secretary of State website. The Small Business Administration also provides resources on their website. You can follow this link or look it up online.

https://www.sba.gov/business-guide/launch-your-busi ness/register-your-business

Remember that the Small Business Administration is a government website that ends in .gov. You don't want to confuse the real site with a commercial copy. You will have to provide sensitive information, and you want to know where it's going.

Once you've filed your name and potentially applied for your tax number (discussed in the next chapter), you've probably taken all the steps you need to get started treating your creative venture like a business. These steps will also impress the IRS and will make them more likely to take you seriously, especially if you're just getting started.

Activity

What will you name your creative endeavor? Choose something that represents your work, check social media availability, and register with the state or states before you take further steps. Jot your notes on the following lines.

40

APPLYING FOR AN EIN OR TIN

hen Kevin was a professional dancer, he handled his finances as a sole proprietorship. However, as he grew older, he danced professionally less, and he opened a dance studio to teach lessons. He knew that with liability issues, he would never want to run a studio as a sole proprietorship. He wanted to create an LLC, taxed as an S corporation, and he learned he needed a tax identification number. His Social Security number wasn't sufficient.

If you are a sole proprietor, you might need an employee identification number (EIN), or you might not. An EIN is a tax identification number that is not your Social Security number. All of us already have Social Security numbers, and if you are simply filing information about your creative endeavor on your personal income tax form on Schedule C, you can probably use your SSN and skip this chapter. But don't stop reading too soon! There are a few circumstances where an EIN is required.

Let's begin with the first and easiest-to-understand reason. If you are any business structure other than a sole proprietor, you probably need an EIN or tax identification number (TIN). This is because your Social Security number is an ID number for you, personally. If you create a business entity, it needs its own tax ID number.

Next, if you file an excise tax return, you need a separate number. You probably don't need to file an excise tax return. Excise tax is paid on items like cigarettes, alcoholic beverages, gasoline, amusement activities like music festivals, and other items unlikely to be part of your creative endeavor. Playing at a music festival doesn't trigger excise tax, but running a festival for a fee would. If you're not sure if you owe excise tax, you need to hire a tax expert to help you with your decisions.

You're more likely to need an EIN or TIN because you have opened a SEP or SIMPLE retirement plan. I talked about these kinds of plans earlier, and they provide a great way to increase your retirement savings if you have sufficient income. SEPs and SIMPLEs require the employer (you) to have an EIN or TIN.

Fortunately, they are very easy to obtain. The IRS provides a step-by-step process that can be accessed on its website at this link:

https://www.irs.gov/businesses/small-businesses-self-employed/employer-id-numbers

Once you are on the page, go to the "Ways to Apply" section. Then, you can click the link or download the form. You will need to know your business entity type and your social security number. Be very careful not to apply twice, or you will have to cancel one of them, and that can be difficult. I know because I made that mistake when I opened my financial firm!

Also, be certain you are working inside the irs.gov webpage. Applications are available on many commercial sites, but you will be providing personal information. I wouldn't be comfortable applying anywhere other than irs.gov or printing the form and sending it to them. I promise it's easy. Even if you read the instructions, which you should, you can complete the process in less than an hour.

This week's task is easy to complete. You might not need an EIN or TIN now, but you probably will eventually. In the meantime, continue to file everything under your Social Security number until your artistic endeavor grows.

Activity

You can use your Social Security number if you are running your creative enterprise as a sole proprietorship. You can also run it under an Employee Identification Number, separate from your SSN. If you want a business structure, like an LLC or S Corporation, you need a Tax Identification Number (TIN). As you are beginning your creative endeavor or looking to formalize it, think about your long-term plans. The fewer numbers associated with your business, the better. Jot your ideas on the following lines.

_____

_____

_____

_____

41

WRITING A BUSINESS PLAN

ndre had started giving piano lessons the previous year, and he was pleased with the number of students he taught. He wasn't sure how many students he would need to supplement the income he earned from accompanying the community opera company. He thought a business plan might help, but he wasn't sure what it should include.

When you start your creative business, you may want to create a business plan. Unless you are seeking funding from someone, the document doesn't have to be formal, and you can make adjustments as you go. Still, having a plan will help you stay organized and may help you consider helpful factors.

Briefly, a business plan shows the strengths and weaknesses of your venture. I know you believe you will succeed. At least I hope you believe that. Otherwise, you are almost doomed to failure. Still, acknowledging potential pitfalls can help you avoid them. Let's look at some of the steps involved in creating a business plan. Because they can be daunting, I'm going to use common descriptions rather than formal language. If you need a high-powered business plan to submit for outside funding, you will want to do additional research.

First, you need a summary of the critical parts of your business. This isn't the place for all the details. Think of it as looking down on the land from a plane. You want to see the big picture.

Next, you will want a more detailed company description, including your business structure (sole prop., S corporation, or LLC), how you can earn money, and any operating limitations, like licensing, that you need to address. This is also where you explain why you are opening your business, and your passion for your talent can be part of the justification. Additionally, you will want to describe how your business is organized. Does it include more people than you? If so, are they officers or workers?

In the following section, you will describe the kinds of things you will do within your business. Include the different ways you can make money while practicing your creative endeavor. How can you be successful in a competitive market?

Related to this is how you are going to find your customers or patrons. Who wants to hire you to perform, commission a painting, or buy your book? How can you find people, both peers and potential purchasers, who love your genre as much as you do? The more you know your market, the more successful you will be. If you operate in a specific niche, learn as much as you can about it.

To find your fans, you are going to need a marketing and sales plan. I know that many people hate marketing, but it's part of any business, even a creative one. We'll talk more about marketing specifics later, but for your business plan, you will want to hit the highlights.

If you are seeking funding, like a grant, the details around the specific request need to be included in the business plan.

Be sure to read carefully the instructions for the funding and address all the requirements.

Whether or not you are seeking funding, your plan will want to include some realistic financial projections. Look to other creatives to see what is reasonable. It's easy to think you will quickly earn money, but making a profit can take some time.

The last part of your plan is the appendix. You may have used resources that you should list. You also want to include your resume and any licenses, permits, or affiliations that make you competitive.

Don't let the complexity of a business plan stop you. Most of the process is thinking through the steps of how you will be structured, who your audience is, and how you will reach them with what they want. Take a step back from your creative endeavor and look at it through a business lens. Working **in** your business is different than working **on** your business. Creating a plan will help your endeavor's long-term chances for success.

Activity

The formality of your business plan will depend on what you are trying to accomplish. You may not need an appendix. You may also need to wait for more information to create realistic financial projections. You must look at your revenue and expenses honestly and take your time. An accurate plan is more important than a quickly developed document full of dreams. Jot your ideas on the following lines.

_____

_____

_____

_____

_____

_____

_____

_____

_____

4 2

JOB OR CAREER?

ulia wanted to be an actor in the world of musical theater, but she knew the path was difficult. Her family was worried she would be financially unstable. Fortunately, a professor suggested she could earn cash by giving singing lessons and working as an artist in residence at a local school. She could pursue her acting career and make a living at the same time.

When I was in high school, I was a classical pianist. In fact, I almost went to college on a piano performance scholarship. My folks were concerned that I would not be able to make a living. Ultimately, I went in a different direction, majoring in English and education before, decades later, I entered finance.

I don't regret my career path. I love everything I do. However, I wish someone would have offered this chapter to both me and my folks. There are many ways of being creative, and the best one is the one that works for you. I want to talk about being creative as a career or a side hustle. I also want to talk about creative-adjacent options that you might not have considered.

No doubt, it's difficult to make your living as a creative. People do it, but it takes talent, sacrifice, and no small amount of luck. If you love your art and you also like to eat, this chapter was written to tell you that whatever path you choose, you've done the right thing for yourself. As you begin to pursue your creative endeavor, you probably have a second job. Maybe that job is designed to provide income alone. You go to work, complete your tasks, collect your check, and then get back to work as a creative. Many creatives follow this path, and it can work well.

Maybe, however, you love your art, but you also find another career interesting. You can have a career in almost any field and be a creative. I love my financial planning business, and I have no intention of closing to pursue writing full-time. I also love to write. I write first thing in the morning and late at night. Then, I manage my financial firm during the day.

I worry that some creative people feel under condemnation if they "sell out." Selling out can mean they created works that are popular and created for purchase, or that they did not pursue their craft with all their heart. I have huge respect and awe for people who can make a living only by following their north star. However, most of us can't make that work financially, and there's nothing wrong with that.

When I rediscovered my love of writing in college, I decided to make money in any way that involved words. I typed (yes, I'm that old). I edited fiction and nonfiction for grammar, and I wrote technical and scholarly articles. One of my best jobs was being a grammar and punctuation editor for atmospheric scientists who spoke English as their second language. I held that side hustle for nine years. I stayed adjacent to the world of writing while getting paid.

The last event that unexpectedly allowed me to write books became possible when I changed careers and entered finance. I saw a need for solid, non-judgmental financial information, and I began writing personal finance books. Those led to a cozy mystery series featuring a financial planner. Now, I write more than I did when I was a creative studies major. However, I still have my day job.

Think outside the box. Look for ways to make money. Don't feel condemned if you need to focus on issues like paying your bills. Never let your creative endeavor totally escape your activities. All creatives are on a different path, and we should celebrate ourselves and those around us.

Activity

I understand the desire to simply practice your creative craft. However, look for some creative-adjacent ways you could also make money. Could you teach or help others improve their skills? Could you work with kids in public schools as an artist in residence? Could you help someone with tedious tasks they don't want to do? Take time to think of all your options, and jot your ideas on the following lines.

_____

_____

_____

_____

43

USEFUL FINANCIAL STATEMENTS

*G*ina had heard the old joke that claimed she must have money because she still had checks. Gina still used checks occasionally, because not everyone took her cash app. She kept up with her bank balance, and nothing ever bounced. Then, one day, she got a notice on her phone that her account had insufficient funds. She discovered that someone had cashed a check she had written to pay for pottery lessons four months ago. Over time, Gina forgot to subtract the amount mentally.

Surely, by this point in the book, you've realized that I'm trying to keep all my information practical and useful for your financial success as a creative. In that spirit, I want to talk about financial statements. Before you close the cover, bear with me a minute. There are some practical reasons why you should keep financial statements, at least informally.

Most importantly, your financial statements are a fast, accurate way to track your financial progress. Additionally, they can provide the data you need to lower your taxes. Although there are many financial statements, I only want to

195

focus on the four I think are most important. Let's get started.

CASH FLOW STATEMENT

Your cash flow is probably the most important document for you to maintain and review regularly. It is exactly what it sounds like—a list of how your money is flowing in and out.

I'm assuming you use a straightforward "cash basis" on your taxes. You can run your finances on a cash basis or an accrual basis. Cash basis means you report your income and expenses when you get the money or pay the bill. Most people do this. Accrual means you list your income and expenses when they are earned or when you promise to pay them. Obviously, you can talk to an accountant about this, but running your creative endeavor using a cash basis is typically the most common way to track your transactions.

To complete your cash flow statement accurately and make your taxes easier, classify the income and expenses you incur using the mandatory IRS tax categories. You can get this list from tax prep software or IRS tax forms available on their website, www.irs.gov. Even if an accountant or tax preparer keeps your books and records for you, be part of the classification process. You need a good understanding of the money you are earning and where that money is going. The easiest way to do this is by keeping or reviewing your own records.

Once you have your income listed at the top of your cash flow statement for the period you're tracking (usually a month) and you've listed your expenses below it, you subtract the expenses from the income. You want the results to be positive!

Other than measuring your profit or loss, your cash flow statement offers other interesting insights. First, even if the number is currently negative and you are operating in the red, are you earning more during each period? Although your income will ebb and flow, you should see steady growth until you reach the level you want. If you aren't there, you may need to add some additional marketing strategies.

Additionally, when you look at all your monthly expenses listed on a page, you can review them and see if you really need them all. It's easy to acquire subscriptions and expenses over time and never realize you don't use them. At least once a year, look closely at what you spend. Do you really need to buy all that stuff? Are you using it? Is there a cheaper or free alternative?

Finally, your cash flow statement is a good way to estimate your tax liability. With a few exceptions, your taxable income is basically what is left after you have paid your bills.

To create an accurate cash flow statement, remember to keep all your receipts along with proof of your income—cash records, copies of checks, credit card summaries, and cash app documents.

DEPRECIATION

Although not a traditional financial statement, understanding depreciation and being able to keep a depreciation table is valuable. Depreciation is a tax treatment that you will probably only use for very expensive purchases, like a computer or a musical instrument. Depreciation is a schedule where you take expenses for a period of years rather than all at once. This allows you to smooth your expenses over time and lower your income in future years when your earnings may be higher. Talk to your CPA about different depreciation periods, called schedules, for different kinds of assets.

Remember you can expense many costly items in a single

year. This would lower your tax liability for that year, although it could result in higher taxes in subsequent years when you didn't have the deduction.

BALANCE SHEET

Cash flow statements are created for a period of time, like a month or year, but balance sheets are calculated for a specific moment in time. Your balance sheet lists all your assets (what you own) and all your liabilities (what you owe) on a page. The difference between assets and liabilities is called "owner's equity," or more informally "net worth." Of course, you want it to be a positive number.

If you need a formal balance sheet, get fancy and categorize your assets as current or fixed. Current assets are cash or items that could be converted to cash within a year. Fixed assets are items that are more difficult to sell, like furniture, equipment, and items necessary to run your business. Fixed assets can also include land and buildings.

Liabilities also have two categories: short-term liabilities and long-term debt. Short-term liabilities are due within a year. They include items like accounts payable or people you owe for a booth at a convention or a venue for music. Short-term liabilities are also the taxes you owe. Long-term debts are bank loans or items you will pay over the course of multiple years.

Even though balance sheets show a single moment in time, you probably don't need to calculate them frequently. Instead, you want to track your changes in owner's equity (net worth) over time. As your owner's equity number increases, you will see your business moving to a more stable financial place. Some tax returns require a balance sheet, so you will want to create at least one per year.

BANK RECONCILIATIONS

I know that reconciling or balancing your bank statement may be something you avoid. However, knowing how much money is truly in your bank account and how that money moves in and out is very important for your financial security.

Primarily, balancing your account will keep you from bouncing checks. One bounced check is not the end of the world, but when you bounce checks on a regular basis, you pay money in fees, lower your credit score, and ding your reputation.

Knowing your bank balance is also helpful as you try to save an emergency fund. Remember that you should have a personal emergency fund and a business emergency fund. That way, if you have an unexpected expense as part of your life or your creative endeavor, you can pay the bill. Balancing your checkbook is a great first step.

You may need to keep additional financial statements other than the ones discussed here. You also might want to talk to a CPA who works with creatives and knows what books and records you should keep. Even if someone helps you keep your books, I want you to take the time to review them. Understanding your financial circumstances lets you make adjustments before you go too far off track.

Activity

Don't let the information in this chapter overwhelm you. You don't need all your financial documents completed today. Set aside one hour a week to work on them. Choose the best time of day for you, and when the hour is over, you can stop until next week. Before you know it, you'll be up to date. Jot your notes on the following lines.

———————————————————————————————————————

———————————————————————————————————————

———————————————————————————————————————

———————————————————————————————————————

———————————————————————————————————————

———————————————————————————————————————

———————————————————————————————————————

———————————————————————————————————————

———————————————————————————————————————

44

EMPLOYMENT TAX

*U*ntil *he started selling his books, Benjamin had never worried about paying taxes on his writing, even though he knew he had the liability. He figured $50 here, $100 there was no big deal. But now, although he couldn't live on his writing income, it was substantial. He had a friend who had majored in accounting and was now a CPA. He warned Benjamin that not only should he pay income taxes, but he should also pay employment taxes. When Benjamin looked confused, his friend explained they were Social Security and Medicare.*

Paychecks are great. Someone else takes care of your taxes and deductions. All you do is answer a few questions, and your employer takes care of everything. You receive your paycheck and go on your way. However, as a creative, often you don't receive a traditional paycheck. It's up to you to be sure you have paid all your liabilities, and often people overlook self-employment tax.

Self-employment tax consists of Social Security and Medicare taxes. The combined rate is 15.3%. Social Security tax is 12.4% and covers old-age, survivors, and disability insurance. Medicare, hospital insurance for senior citizens, takes the other 2.9 percent

In 2025, the first $176,100 of your income is subject to Social Security tax, and all of your income is always subject to Medicare.

When I talk to people about Social Security, some roll their eyes and claim that the benefit won't be there, so why should they pay it? The easy answer is if you don't, you will owe interest and potentially face criminal prosecution. In 2024, if you earn $400 or more in self-employment income or more than $108.28 in church employee income, you owe self-employment tax.

I genuinely believe our government will ensure the benefit. I know it's a political hot button right now, but all politicians have one thing in common: they want to be re-elected. And from a cynical perspective, senior citizens vote in higher percentages than many other demographics.

Full retirement age, the age at which you receive your full Social Security amount, might be raised, but the fundamental benefit will continue. Additionally, to solve the underfunding issue, Congress could eliminate the income phaseout. If all income were subject to Social Security tax, funding would be instantly solved.

As you calculate your employment tax, remember that, as a self-employed creative, you are the equivalent of both the employer and the employee. (We talked about this earlier when we calculated net income from self-employment.) However, you get an income tax deduction for the half you pay as an employer.

One advantage of being self-employed is that you usually do not need to pay unemployment insurance as part of your employment taxes. Because you cannot fire yourself, unemployment insurance is not an issue. If you have employees, talk to a CPA to see the unemployment insurance require-ments in your state.

You pay self-employment taxes at the same time you make quarterly income tax payments. To process these payments, you must have a Social Security number or an individual taxpayer identification number (EIN or TIN). We discussed how to get this number earlier. Additionally, you can employ a bookkeeper or purchase a payroll service. Although I know you want to save money, I find a payroll service helpful. All I do is enter the amount of income, and the company calculates everything. As much as you can, you should focus on your strengths and use services to assist you with what causes you stress.

Activity

When you are a self-employed creative, keeping up with all the taxes can be difficult. You don't want to forget to pay employment taxes. Not only could you get in trouble and be assessed a fine, but also, when you were older, you wouldn't have the benefits. Jot your notes on the following lines.

_____

_____

_____

_____

45

PRICING YOUR WORK

*J*ustin *looked at the paintings scattered around him.*
He was excited and scared at the same time. He knew
when he placed them on the white walls of his new
studio, he needed to include prices. He loved his work, but he knew
he didn't have a big following yet. His pieces would be on the lower
end of the range, but what was the range?

One of the most difficult things to do as a creative is price
your work. You want to earn a reasonable amount of money,
but you don't want to price your work too high or too low.
Considering a few things may make the process easier.

First, determine the actual cost of your creation. Does it
take special supplies? Do you need to purchase equipment or
rent time in another location to use their tools? Include not
only the immediate costs but also consider the expense of
using equipment that will wear out. Do you use a kiln? A
laptop? A musical instrument? You must eventually replace
items like these, and you want to prorate the costs and save
the replacement price a little at a time.

Next, how much is your time worth? This is a difficult
determination, especially if you enjoy what you do. You may

not feel like creating your art is drudgery. I hope you don't. However, you still need to be compensated for your time. If you don't know how to proceed with this part of the process, keep reading.

You may not be aware that recommended pricing strategies exist for different creative genres. Before you decide what to charge, you need to look at what is recommended in your field. However, I suspect default pricing may not be very successful. In different parts of the country, the same job pays different amounts of money. Doubtless, the price of creation also varies over geographic regions. Still, I think it's important to know the average pricing in your field. It gives you a place to begin.

However, beyond anything else, I think looking at equivalent work in your region will give you the best idea of how to price your work. Your more experienced friends can help you with this. Of course, name recognition of an artist can help drive prices, as can genres that have become trendy. However, pricing that is equivalent to your competition will probably provide you with the most financial success.

If your works don't sell at that price, consider different options. Could you create some smaller pieces that might sell more easily because they are automatically less expensive? Could you sell prints? Short stories? Creating more inexpensive works may help build dedicated fans.

Additionally, go back to the value of your time. Your time is important, and you should never consider underestimating it. However, would you be willing to work for a little less if it would help you make a sale? I can't answer that question. You could try lowering the price and seeing what happens.

If you don't want to directly lower the price, you could offer a deal. You could make the first book of your series less expensive to hook your readers. Then, charge more for the following books. You could offer one small free painting if someone purchases two larger ones.

You may need to become creative in how you offer deals and sales. The advantage of this strategy is you haven't actually lowered your prices. As you gain more publicity, you can offer fewer discounts and increase your revenue.

Too many times, we don't think what we create has value. Don't make the mistake of selling yourself short. If you want to treat your creative endeavor like a business, you need to create the potential for making a profit.

Activity

Look at the metrics specific to your discipline for pricing your work, but don't stop there. Calculate how much it will take you to create your piece, the value of your time, and the price of equivalent work. Jot your notes on the following lines.

_____

_____

_____

_____

_____

46

MARKETING

*G*loria was desperate to drive business to her online jewelry store. Once people found her, they usually bought something and later returned for additional purchases. She had a social media presence, but she felt people didn't engage as much as she wanted. A friend offered to split a booth at their local farmer's market. The day was beautiful, and people were having fun. Soon, they flocked around the booth and bought their jewelry. Gloria and her friend alternated taking pictures of each other with the crowds, and they posted them on social media, tagging the market. It took time and consistency, but her likes, comments, and sales increased.

When you ask many creatives what they hate the most about their craft, they often say promotion or marketing. Talking about yourself can be embarrassing. Asking people to hire you for a gig or role or to purchase your creations can feel awkward. Yet, without a marketing plan, you may find yourself either not increasing your fan base or spending too much money on items that don't work.

As you create a marketing plan, you want to try to reach as many people as possible. When Willie Sutton was asked why he robbed banks, he answered, "Because that's where the money is." Now, Willie's behavior might have been questionable, but his motivation was accurate. You want to put your efforts where you will have the most success. We'll talk about social media in the next chapter, but marketing is more than a Facebook account.

The most important part of your marketing plan should be a followers' list. The people on this list should provide their email addresses and, perhaps other contact information. They should be fine with your sending them information about your events and releases. Gather names through sign-in sheets or QR codes at events or online forms on your social media. You can also subscribe to services that help you gather names through contests and fan interaction. Remember any time you pay for a service, monitor the progress to be sure it's worth the money. Once you begin to gather fans, their friends may become even a wider audience.

Having an audience allows you to create an effective newsletter. Your musings should be fun and entertaining and maybe include a contest giveaway. You want your fans to know where you will be appearing, signing, or showing. You want to let them see a little about you. It's fine to maintain your privacy, but you want your followers to know enough about you to be able to bond. Maybe you also like to cook or garden. You could include a tip in each newsletter. You don't want to bombard your followers, but you should probably try to write one newsletter a month. You want them to remember you without making them crazy. Remember to make it easy for them to opt out of future letters through an "unsubscribe" button. You're supposed to provide one, and the cleaner you provide everything, the more likely they are to refer you, not leave you.

You will also want to create a website. Today, almost every creative has a site. You should include a calendar of your events and pictures. If you write a blog, include it on your site or provide the link. Also, include ways to access all your social media. Keep the content fresh and change things up periodically to reflect how your creative endeavor is growing.

If you attend conventions or conferences, are there fans? If there are, you might want to sponsor an event or provide a basket for a charity auction. Having such a presence will gain people's attention.

Try to participate in any local events. Often, your initial fan base will come from your hometown. Festivals, art walks, and even farmer's markets can give you an opportunity to get in front of people. Additionally, these local occasions are often not expensive.

A second way to participate locally is to sponsor a community event. Compared to other kinds of traditional advertising, this can be inexpensive. For a small contribution (in advertising terms), the event may be willing to include you in their promotional material and call out your name during the event. I discovered this secret years ago with my financial firm. I prefer sponsoring to advertising. I like the connection it creates between my business and the arts community, and I love being mentioned rather than making a direct ask for clients. However, there's nothing wrong with asking for business!!

Before you begin spending money, decide in advance your marketing budget. Be wary of expensive marketing schemes. Often, the only people who make money with these are the folks you paid to be included.

I've made this mistake, myself. Years ago, I bought an ad at a local gym because I was told that community leaders were members. Although the leaders were there, they weren't looking for a financial planner. They just wanted to go walk, work out, or swim. I spent a lot of money for no return. Many people will contact you with marketing ideas for you to purchase. Take time and decide if the opportunity will truly be beneficial. Talk to your friends to see if they have had luck with similar purchases.

Don't view marketing as a chore. It's fun to share what you are doing with the world. If no one knows you exist, they can't see how awesome you are!

Activity

First, determine your marketing budget. Then, decide how your fans would find you the easiest. Create a presence in those locations, and don't give up quickly. Nothing is magical, and building a business takes time. However, you'll never get there without marketing. Jot your notes on the following lines.

47

SOCIAL MEDIA

attie loved playing acoustic guitar at local restaurants and clubs. She had a following, but she wanted more people to listen to her perform. Her tribe told her she should work on her social media presence, but she was overwhelmed. Finally, a friend suggested she focus on only one or two platforms. Without needing to manage six or seven places to post, Mattie spent her time on the sites she liked. Soon, she expanded her fan base and her audience.

Recently, I was at a writing retreat, and the group discussion centered on what people hated the most about writing. Social media won, hands down. Over time, I've come to enjoy marketing, but even I get overwhelmed, feeling like I should do everything and be everywhere.

And yet, social media provides us with the easiest venues to get our creative ventures in front of a potentially large audience. Unfortunately, creatives sometimes tell me they don't want anything to do with it. If you agree with them, that's fine. However, social media is almost inescapable if you want to treat your creative work as a business.

Maintaining social media accounts has advantages. Not

only can most marketing be free, but the price of promotions, like Facebook ads, is quite reasonable. Additionally, if
you are trying to convince the IRS that your writing is a
business, having a booming social media presence goes a
long way. However, if the process seems daunting, I've got
some ideas to make it easier.

First, take time to study the different platforms. Most
importantly, learn about their demographics and compare
them to your fan base. You may want to branch out from
your strongest demographic, but you also should include it.
There is too much social media to maintain accounts everywhere. Feel free to eliminate platforms you don't like.

Additionally, ask yourself some more personal questions.
Where do you enjoy reading posts, especially those about
your craft? Which platforms lend themselves to your
medium? Where are your friends? You don't have to reinvent
the mousetrap. Find out what others in your genre are
successfully using.

If you haven't already, open an account and begin to
follow people you like. Follow your creative friends, but also
follow other artists. Not only do you want to see what they
are doing, but you also want to see how they are sharing
their information. Study the posts of pages you enjoy. Why
do you find them engaging? Don't try to become someone
else, but you might be able to gain some useful insights.

I'm often asked if someone should have a personal social
media page and a separate creative or business page. Social
media can be overwhelming, but if you keep a separate artist
page, you can focus on those pursuits. That way, you exclude
the pictures of your dinner, your latest trip to the beach, and
selfies with friends! If you do create a business page, I've found
you probably ought to have a personal page, as well. Not only
do many sites require it, but your friends will start tagging you

from your business page. I like keeping a little space between my personal life and my business endeavors, but it's your choice. Remember, once it's on social media, it lives forever!

Of course, the big issue with social media is sharing often enough. Remember to include different types of posts. You can like, share, and create. Free or inexpensive software makes creating fabulous posts easy.

If you're short on ideas, look for posts that would be interesting to someone who likes the content of your page. For example, look up a calendar of famous creatives' birthdays. Then, you can create a post celebrating the day. Also, don't forget to include local events related to your craft, and create invitations for your fans if you are part of the activities.

As you post, don't forget to include any hashtags that might apply. Hashtags are the keyboard symbol # plus a keyword about your post. Use popular or trending tags to get your posts in front of more eyes. For example, if you do a Halloween post, include #Halloween, along with any other hashtags that seem relevant. Maximize the value of each post you make.

Even though experts often say you should post once a day, that can become overwhelming, especially if you get caught up in the social media rabbit hole. Instead, use free scheduling software. Some sites include it, but third-party software works well, too. Then, create and schedule your posts one day a week or twice a month. You can schedule different platforms at the same time. And finally, don't forget your "thank you" posts. Without your fans, pursuing your creative world would be difficult.

If all of this sounds like too much, just start at the beginning. Choose your favorite social media platform and begin posting there. Add a hashtag to increase your visibility. As you get more followers and likes, you may find you begin to enjoy the process.

Activity

Do you have a social media presence for your creative activities? If you know you need to expand your social media presence, focus on sites you enjoy. Also, research where your fans receive their information. You don't need to be everywhere, but you do need a vibrant social media presence. Jot your ideas on the following lines.

48

CONTRACTS

*S*usan *was so excited when she sold her first book that she signed the contract without looking at the details. The book was a big success, and Susan received a movie offer. When she read her contract more closely, she discovered the publisher would receive most of the revenue from the film. She wished she had read the contract before she signed it.*

Congratulations! You've received a contract! Someone thinks you're wonderful, and they want to pay you. Reading the contract, however, is daunting. Most contracts are many pages long and likely contain words you can't define. The first and most important piece of advice in this chapter is to hire an attorney in your field to help you read the contract and not make any catastrophic errors that will haunt you for years. Of course, if this is your first contract, you may not have enough money to hire an attorney. What should you do then?

To begin, I am also not an attorney, and nothing in this chapter is legal advice. Instead, it's a combination of things I've experienced and recommendations from creative friends of mine who also negotiate contracts. The resources I found didn't have as many good ideas as my friends did.

First, read the contract during the time of day you think the best. If you are a morning person, get up, make coffee, and dive in. If you are a night person, have a non-alcoholic beverage and begin to read. Don't try to read the entire contract in one sitting. When material is difficult, at some point, you are likely just to nod and proceed. You can overlook major issues with that strategy.

As you are reading, highlight every word you don't know, then go look them up. Do not sign a document that contains words you don't understand. Additionally, as you review it, look for the following components.

- What are the terms of the contract? In other words, how long does it last? When do the rights revert back to you? Be certain that the contract follows industry best practices.
- If the contract covers multiple items, check how any advances are paid. You don't want to be trapped into only receiving royalties after all items have earned back their advances. This type of contract is called a "basket." Earning an advance and subsequent royalties on each component might be advantageous.
- Look for artificial intelligence (AI) clauses. Now that so much software automatically includes an AI component, be careful not to use a tool that violates the contract accidentally.
- Look at different media rights. What do they keep? What do you maintain? Do you keep gaming rights? In some areas, this is a huge source of revenue that is often overlooked. Do they own the

world you built? If you leave the company, can you take the world with you?

- Does the contract require that you offer the company an option on your next book or other creative endeavor?
- If you are writing a book or have another creative endeavor with a front piece, do you own the cover?
- If you are writing a book, does the contract specify "print on demand"? This might control the availability of books if your source sells out.
- Does the contract contain a "use it or lose it" clause that gives you back rights that are not used?
- How can you exit the contract? Can you break it early?

Your contract will contain many more components than I covered in this chapter. It's important that you read every line.

Of course, if your contract cannot be modified, you need to make a decision. Do you want the contract, or do you say no? Some set contracts offer good terms and can be signed. Others might need a second look.

Finally, even if you have retained an attorney, talk to friends who have already received contracts in your field. Ask them about any pitfalls you should avoid. I know you are eager to sign and move forward, but a little effort today can prevent years of heartache.

Activity

Congratulations on your contract! If you can afford one, enlist the assistance of an attorney or agent. Otherwise, talk to creatives in your genre about the terms of their contracts.

Be careful not to give away more rights or revenue than industry standards. Jot your ideas on the following lines.

49

REPRESENTATION

*J*ackson liked to hang out with creatives. Sometimes, he was with his own tribe of actors, but he had other friends who were writers, dancers, and visual artists. As they all talked about the need for representation, Jackson realized that different kinds of artists used the same words in different ways. Between disciplines, not all agents and managers did the same things. He realized that if he needed guidance, he should talk to other dancers.

Many creatives need some kind of representation, whether it's an agent, manager, publicist, or someone else. Although talking about choosing the right person is an important part of treating your endeavor like a business, various artistic disciplines deal with representation in different ways. Some people help with bookings and contracts. Others negotiate deals, while still others serve in different capacities.

Because of the complexity of this topic, I want to talk about it as an overview, giving you areas to investigate. Especially here, you will need to talk to friends in your industry. Who are they hiring? Why are they working with them?

Don't ask these questions right after you meet someone. Instead, become an active part of your local creative community. Once you are attending events, you can find ways of asking questions without looking pushy or creepy.

Still, I can discuss some basic things here. If you are new in your craft and you receive a proposal of representation, you may be so excited that you agree without looking at the details. Some offers are legitimate, while others are less reputable. Be very careful before you sign anything.

First, all business agreements must involve a contract. Read it word for word at the time of day when you are the sharpest, as I suggested in the last chapter. Take your time, and don't read when you're tired. Of course, you can't sit on an offer for an extended period, but you certainly should be able to take a couple of days. Look up every word you don't know. And finally, talk to more experienced friends in the industry. Do they think the terms of the representation are reasonable?

Outside of the fairness of the agreement, be sure you understand what services you will be receiving and what you are supposed to provide. I see creatives who get angry with people in the industry for not delivering. Sometimes, the problem is the representative, but other times, the problem is a lack of understanding on the part of the creative. The creative is expecting the representative to do something he or she doesn't provide or can't deliver.

For example, when a writer has a publicist, both parties need to understand what marketing services will be provided by the publicist and what the writer must do. If the writer is unwilling or unable to complete the tasks, he or she shouldn't use that publicist.

Continuing with our writing metaphor, if a publishing contract is reasonable and the writer isn't receiving as much money in royalties as he or she anticipated, the problem may be a lack of sales. The author may need to increase their own marketing efforts. In today's world, it's up to most creatives to do the legwork.

Now, sometimes, the fault is the representation. Many publishing scams exist where fraudulent companies promise to sell your books, usually for a hefty fee. Again, talk to the people in your tribe. These companies are usually well known, and your friends can help you avoid them.

Representation can take another dark path. Sometimes, people who you hire to help end up stealing from you. We've all heard of giant celebrities scammed by those closest to them. Don't let that happen to you. Stay engaged with all parts of your creative business.

The financial side may be your least favorite part, but that's exactly where most of the fraud occurs. Make sure your reported income roughly matches what you think you earned. You should also have a basic idea of your expenses. If things don't make sense, ask questions. Most representatives are honest, but you should be careful.

Representation is exciting. An offer makes you feel like your endeavor is legitimate—that you're a "real" creative. Representation is also necessary. But the world can be full of pitfalls and problems. Your best resources will come from your tribe, but reading your legal documents and monitoring your financial records will go a long way toward keeping you safe.

Activity

Once you reach a certain level of professionalism, you will need representation to help with your career path, booking opportunities, and contract negotiations. This area is fraught with fraud and confusion. Your best plan is to join professional organizations in your own discipline and learn the ins and outs of this part of your creative business. Jot your ideas on the following lines.

_____

_____

_____

_____

_____

_____

_____

_____

_____

50

COPYRIGHTS

J orge loved writing folk songs. He scored for voice, piano, guitar, and other Appalachian folk music instruments. His group had a huge following, and everyone loved his music. He hadn't bothered to copyright anything, and he mentioned it to a friend. His friend was horrified and told him he needed to complete the process immediately. Jorge didn't know where to begin.

There are different ways of protecting your creative work, and one of the most common is copyright. Copyright protects the creators of "original works of authorship." They include many kinds of endeavors: writing, music, drama, pictures, movies, and other categories.

Copyrights are filed with the Copyright Office, and a fantastic resource for creatives is www.copyright.gov/ engage/. On this page, they give the basics of copyright, which I will also discuss in this chapter. The real magic of their site, however, is how they offer links to specific information for different kinds of creative endeavors—music, photography, writers, visual artists, and graphic artists.

Copyright allows the owner to make copies of their work,

distribute them to sell, and display or perform their work publicly, along with other rights. Copyright doesn't protect ideas, choreography (although they would cover a video of the choreography), titles, familiar images, small changes to an existing copyright, or a list of ingredients or contents.

You can claim a copyright if you are the creator of the item. If your work is published in an anthology, your copyright is your contribution. If someone else hires you to create something, the copyright belongs to them, not you.

As we discussed in the estate section, you can pass your copyright to your heirs, and it will generally exist for seventy years after your death.

Registering your item with the Copyright Office is strongly recommended. However, their website explains that your copyright technically exists the minute you create your work and preserve it in a tangible form perceptible directly or with the aid of a device. Some people advocate creating a "poor person's" copyright by mailing yourself a copy that has the date in the stamp cancellation. However, that process makes me nervous. Going through the Copyright Office is a much safer option.

Your official copyright exists when the Office receives your application, a copy of what you are registering, and the fee. The fees vary but can be found by following the path on the website I gave you earlier in the chapter. Depending on your work, most of the fees are less than $100.

Once your copyright is registered, the Copyright Office provides specific language you can use to add to copies of your work. Be sure that you copy it correctly.

If you are using a traditional publisher, you should retain the copyright to your material even if you don't prepare the document. For example, on the inside of the books I have traditionally published, I am listed as the owner of the copyright. The publisher includes the language and does not retain the copyright for itself. As you are seeking out companies or organizations to help you share your creations with the world, be sure that you retain your copyright. The topic should be addressed in any contract, so read carefully before you sign anything.

If you are treating your creative endeavor as a business, you should either apply for the copyright yourself or ensure that your publisher is completing that step for you. Not only does it offer further artistic protection, but you are also showing the IRS that you are serious.

Activity

If you have a creative work you can copyright, get additional information about the process at www.copyright.gov/engage/. Be sure you are on the governmental copyright website. Jot your notes on the following lines.

_____

_____

_____

_____

_____

THE LIBRARY OF CONGRESS

*J*ill was excited to be an indie author. She enjoyed having complete artistic control over her short stories. When she finished her first anthology, she got a copyright and posted the book to several online sites. When her friend Jaxon, a poet, bought her book and began to read it, he asked her if she had registered her work with the Library of Congress. Jill said she hadn't thought about doing that and asked Jaxon if she could do it then. He said no, she needed to register her book before publication.

This chapter is mostly for my writer friends and, specifically, for my indie author friends. When you traditionally publish, you don't have to worry about registering your work at sites where you might want it to be found. However, indies don't have that luxury, and registering your indie-published book with the Library of Congress (LOC) is a task you may not have considered. However, librarians use the LOC to find books. Having an LOC listing provides credibility, and although not a copyright, you are strengthening your ownership claims.

Before we talk about the details of registering with the

Library of Congress, if you are only published as an e-book without a paper copy, you cannot register with the LOC. The e-books they include are mostly works that have been previously published but need to be read electronically to protect the manuscript. Copies of newspapers, government reports, and other previously printed materials are also available at the LOC.

Additionally, I want to apologize to other types of creatives reading this book. Although film and music are both cataloged in the Library of Congress, the works must be at least ten years old and, according to their website, "hold an enduring importance in American culture." They only accept twenty-five works in each genre a year.

As one more disclaimer, if you are a traditionally published author, your publisher is taking care of all of this for you. You don't need to take any steps to have your book included in the Library of Congress. If you want clarification, talk to your editor or, if you have one, your literary agent.

However, the world of indie authors is growing every day. Many authors are choosing to take control of their creative works, and the Library of Congress has recognized this fact.

If you are an indie author with printed books, you need to know one important thing about having your work included in the Library of Congress. You must submit your application **before** your book's release date. Fortunately, the process isn't difficult.

First, go to the Library of Congress Author Portal, which you can access from their PrePub page: https://www.loc.gov/programs/prepub-book-link/about-this-program/. At the top of this page, you can find a link for user guides. You will want to download the one for authors and self-publishers. On the same page, you will find the author portal link.

Open the user guide to follow the process of creating your account and submit information about your book. Once you have completed the process and they have approved it, don't forget to send them paper copies of your book after publication.

Having your book registered in the Library of Congress is exciting. Remember that on your next trip to Washington, DC, if you contact the library in advance, they can show you the copy! For a little effort, you can increase your book's visibility, especially with librarians, enhance your claim of ownership, and do something that's just cool.

Activity

Explore the Library of Congress website, https://www.loc.gov/programs/prepub-book-link/about-this-program/, to learn how to register your creative work. Jot some notes on the following lines.

_____

_____

_____

_____

_____

CREATING AN ONLINE STORE

*J*eanie was a tremendous seamstress, and she loved to sell her creations. However, going to shows was time-consuming, and bad weather impacted her sales. She wanted to create an online store on a crafting website. However, she had never done anything like that, and she wasn't sure where to begin.

If you are a visual artist, jewelry maker, seamstress, or other creator of tangible things, you may want to open an online store. Do some research first and decide which platforms would give you the most visibility and lead to the most sales. You can link your online store to your website and, potentially, social media sites. You can also create posts showcasing your store on these sites, as well.

Once you have chosen an online platform, find articles that describe the store's creation process. I am going to discuss some general considerations in this chapter, but you will want to study the process specifically.

I'm assuming you already know what you want to sell. If you don't, you need to decide that first, as keeping focused will help you be successful. If you're just starting to create, you might want to attend some local shows and events before you build an online presence. You may be surprised at which items sell the best.

Once you know what you're selling, you need a store with a great name. Discuss your idea for the name with other creatives, and maybe even poll your followers with two or three of your best ideas. Choosing the right name is key to your business' success, and don't forget to check with your state to ensure the name is available. An attorney can also help you do a national search.

You will want to decide how to take payments. Again, this may be a function of who is hosting your store. Even if you haven't set up payment methods yet, they aren't difficult. You probably want to offer two or three, because not all your clients will want to purchase things the same way.

One of the most important parts of your online store is how you photograph and display your goods. The pictures of your creations impact how well they sell. If you can afford it, hire a professional photographer. If you can't, look at other sites to see how they display their items. I have a bias toward simple layouts, but it's your store. Before you post the pictures on your site, you might run them by your friends again. You don't want to turn people off by not displaying things well.

Once your items are listed, use descriptive tags that will draw people to them. The tags should never be misleading, but they should include topics that your patrons would enjoy. Don't try to do them all in one sitting. Take one item (or type of item) a day and work on your description and tags. Just like hashtags are key to social media success, tags are vital to people finding your products on crafting websites.

As I discussed in an earlier chapter, pricing your items can be tricky. You need to incorporate all the expenses associated with your creative process. You also need to decide how much your time is worth. How much are equivalent items on the site? You don't want to be much more expensive or cheap than your competition.

Now that your store is open, you need to market, market, market. Employ resources available from your site host, social media posts, and cross-posting with friends. Offer seasonal promotions, sales, and other incentives. Everyone loves a deal. Just make sure that you keep your business profitable for you.

From an administrative perspective, using a selling platform makes your life easier. The site will keep up with your purchases and handle the details of your sales tax. Even though you lose a percentage of your profit when you use a platform, the ease of handling the business and tax side of your venture may be worth the cost.

Finally, once you have a sale, fill it promptly and try to exceed your customers' expectations. I've received short, handwritten notes thanking me for my purchase. In this day of robot voices, the personal touch goes a long way.

Opening an online store has many considerations. Take time to think through the details before you begin the process, and don't go "live" until you've dealt with as many items as you can imagine. Then, keep the site fresh and always look to improve. You get to be creative, make money, and have the satisfaction of clients who keep coming back for more purchases.

Activity

If you want to open an online presence on a crafting website, your best first step is to read their instructions. Make sure you understand and agree with their terms and conditions before you bother creating a business name or photographing the items you plan to sell. Assuming you want to proceed, follow their steps and the ideas in this chapter. Jot your ideas on the following lines.

_____

_____

_____

_____

_____

_____

_____

_____

_____

FINAL THOUGHTS

Congratulations! You did it! You finished reading a finance book! I hope you found the information helpful. Remember that you can find more information on my website, www. peggydoviak.com. I include an "Updates" page where I will keep the information in the book current. You can also always check changes to contribution limits and income phaseouts through a quick online search.

Additionally, my website provides my calendar of upcoming events, my blog, and pictures. You can also buy my books! I write personal finance and cozy mysteries, and I'd love for you to check them out.

Thank you so much for buying my book and taking the time to read it. Without my readers, writing isn't much fun.

Be Prosperous!

Peggy Doviak

ACKNOWLEDGMENTS

Tremendous thanks to all my creative friends who took time out of their busy lives to help me with the topics in this book. Your recommendations made this book much better than it could have been without your feedback and support! I hope you find it useful.

Thank you, RC Davis, for encouraging me to start the path of writing personal finance.

Thank you, Nancy Berland, for encouraging my writing for so many years, helping position my writing career, editing, and being an all-around great friend.

Thank you, Molly Baron, for the awesome cover! Didn't she do a great job?

Thank you, Priya Bhakta and KaliOka Press, for your help in bringing this to life.

Thank you to all my writer friends who have invited me to share financial information with their readers. Sheila Roberts, I love the events you schedule for us. Marie Bostwick, thank you for the blogging opportunities. Lori Hayes, thank you for the interview. Pam Binder, thank you for the speaking opportunities. Thanks to my Kauai writing buddies for answering so many questions. And finally, thanks also to the Oklahoma writing groups, OWFI and Tornado Alley SinC, who have offered speaking invitations once they knew about the book.

Thank you to my family, both by blood and by love, who have been so supportive. Special thanks to my aunt,

Margaret Beggs, for all your support and great meals! And thanks to my angelic husband, Richard Doviak, who told me I had to write this book series. All my love.

ABOUT THE AUTHOR

Peggy Doviak's path to finance began when her mother got taken to the cleaners by an unscrupulous stockbroker. Peggy became so angry that she abandoned her background in English and Education to pursue a career in financial planning.

Now, Peggy is a CERTIFIED FINANCIAL PLANNER™ practitioner, radio and podcast host, and best-selling author of two award-winning personal finance books. She also has written one cozy mystery with a second to be released in 2025. When she's not working, Peggy loves to travel, read, and spend time with her two horses and two cats.

Peggy's first two books, *52 Weeks to Prosperity* and *52 Weeks to Well-Being* are available through online sources or at your local bookstore. Learn more about Peggy at her website.

www.askpeggy.com